REMINISCENCES OF
BARIL LAKE AND CAMP OWAKONZE

DONALD WILMARTH ICKES
1996

TABLE OF CONTENTS

TABLE OF CONTENTS i

INTRODUCTION 1

EARLY HISTORY OF BARIL LAKE 1

FUR TRADE AND WESTWARD COLONIZATION...2

THE BEGINNINGS OF THE CAMP 3

DUKE CHILDS...4

BUILDING OWAKONZE 6

SPORTS AND ACTIVITIES 11

CANOE TRIPS 14

TRANSPORTATION 15

KITCHEN 19

COMMUNICATION 20

CAMP OWAKONZE, LTD...23

ADVANCED TRIPS...25

CARETAKERS AND NEIGHBORS..26

ICKES' FOLLY AND OTHER PROJECTS 32

COMPILATION OF THE HISTORY OF OWAKONZE...34

INTRODUCTION

This narrative was a collaborative effort between Don Ickes and his children who pushed him relentlessly the last couple of years of Don's life. Don passed away in January of 1995. His last years were difficult due to illness and the realization that he could no longer do many of the things that he once loved. It was with much nagging and prodding that we got him to write most of this document. Alison sat with him for more than four hours one day with a huge box of old photographs and papers from camp and made him label them. Most of the written text is what Don wrote in 1994. He had been yanked into the technological era by the computer. This was a man who just loved mimeographs and facsimile machines! He did well on the computer as long as he stuck to typing. The concept of making files was beyond him, so that every time he worked on the history he would create a new file. The result was six separate discs with countless files and several printed copies of most of them. It took a bit of wandering through the files and reading the papers to figure out what changes had been made on each. Some of what Don wrote has been edited, but, for the most part, this is his account of "his" camp.

In reality, this narrative only touches a portion of what Baril Lake and Owakonze were and continue to be. There does not seem to be an effective way to convey to the readers what a remarkable place and what extraordinary people have been involved in the growth and development of Owakonze. For readers this who have had the good fortune to spend time on Baril Lake, this will evoke bits of memories and feelings and perhaps even smells. This history will never be complete, but this document is an attempt to gather some of it in. As with everything, time changes and things move on. When Don wrote this Father Paul Sheridan was still the active director of Boy's Hope Owakonze. In 1996, however, he left Owakonze to other directors and was assigned to a position in Australia. There is no doubt that Owakonze has not left him where ever he is.

EARLY HISTORY OF BARIL LAKE

At first glimpse, Baril Lake appears to be a small lake located in western Ontario, Canada. At the western end of the lake is the Canadian National Railroad (CNR) railroad line. At one time, the name Owakonze could be found on maps as a stop on the route. In fact, the train would stop twice a day in the 1940s and 1950s; once from the east and once from the west. On some of the better regional maps Baril Lake is labeled. More often, however, it only shows up as a small lake to the west of the much larger Lac Des Mille Lacs. Upon closer inspection, and a bit of research, it becomes clear that this little lake is actually a gem of physical beauty and history which only a few lucky people have had the chance to see and know.

Baril Lake played an important role in the formative years of more than a thousand young men who were fortunate enough to be a part of Camp Owakonze, a wilderness canoeing camp that was founded in the early 1920's and has continued in one form or another to the present day. It is likely that many of the young men never gave much thought to the physical environment of Baril Lake, or to the historical significance of the area, or of Owakonze. It is a fact that most went away from the wilderness camp with a bank full of memories and new skills that they would keep and draw upon for the remainder of their lives. This narrative is an attempt to gather the rich history of the lake and of the camp.

The lake is approximately ten miles in length and runs essentially east to west. It is a very deep, cold lake, although it has a number of rocky reefs that surface in unexpected places. The shoreline is mostly rocky (this is the Canadian Shield region), with a few, isolated sandy areas that form small beaches when the water level is low. The lake is narrow, a mile or so across the main part of it, with several large bays. The altitude is approximately 1,700 feet. From the vicinity of Baril Lake, the water sheds in three directions; north to Hudson's Bay, southeast to Lake Superior and west to Lake Of The Woods. There are several islands located throughout the lake, some many acres, others much smaller.

White and Norway pine, birch, poplar, balsam and spruce are the common trees throughout the lake and islands. Baril Lake is the natural home of lake trout, whitefish, pickerel and great northern pike. The lake was stocked with walleyed pike in 1928 and speckled trout in 1929; in later years bass were added. The region is home to wolf, fox, fisher, martin, mink, beaver, moose, bear and deer. Most of these animals are no longer as plentiful as they were in the 1920's. Hunting, trapping and the encroachment and logging by man has depleted the numbers of animals. There are also several types of ducks, gulls, loons, hawks and small song birds, owls and the occasional bald eagle that are at home on the lake.

FUR TRADE AND WESTWARD COLONIZATION

Early fur traders used the lake as a route for the Northwest Company and the Hudson's Bay Company. It was also on the route of what was called the Riel Rebellion expedition under Colonel Garnet Wolseley. The Riel Rebellion took place at Ft. Garry (now Winnipeg). The Canadian federal government dispatched troops under Colonel Wolseley from Ottawa by water through the Great Lakes to the Grand Portage on Lake Superior. From there, they traveled by canoe and barges which were built to carry the men through the larger lakes out to Winnipeg. Approximately 1,600 men and 250 boats used the route to reach Winnipeg, some 400 or more miles from Lake Superior.

Still later, in an attempt to colonize the western parts of Canada, Baril Lake was on the main water route to the western prairies. The route was known as the Dawson Trail, somewhat akin to the Oregon Trail in the United States. The Canadian government sent four men, including Simon Dawson, to plan a waterway from Lake Superior westward. The first survey of what was called the Canadian Red River Exploring

Expedition was done in 1854, but it was another decade or more before it became a reality. Colonists from the eastern part of Canada were brought to the Grand Portage and then through the lakes across the portages, including Baril Lake, westward to the flat country, which is now Manitoba, to settle and build farms. Relics from this migration can occasionally still be found on Baril Lake. Canadian Confederation occurred on July 1, 1867, by which time the Dawson Trail route had been completed. By 1875, it's peak year, some 2000 people used the waterway, with several thousand more following the route until about 1880, when railroad transportation in the United States rendered it's further use impractical. It is probable that abandoned log cabins on the two islands that would be occupied by Camp Owakonze were built during these times.

Shortly before the turn of the century Baril Lake was the site of logging operations. First-growth white pine and spruce were cut along it's shores and moved by means of an endless cable known as an "alligator" powered by a large steam engine. The logs were hauled out of the east end of the lake and sent down a chute into Lac Des Mille Lacs. From there, with the aid of steam tugs, massive log booms were towed to the far northeast end of Mille Lacs at Savanne, where they were loaded onto the Canadian Pacific Railroad which had been completed by then. The remains of the "alligator" with it's cable and steam engine can be seen today at the east end of Baril Lake, along with what is left of one of the Dawson Trail barges built on the lake.

THE BEGINNINGS OF THE CAMP

Early in the century Camp Minocqua was started in Minocqua, Wisconsin by three men who served as Directors; J.P. Sprague, MD was a surgeon at the Universities of Illinois and Chicago, Professor A.E. Buck was from Grinell College in Iowa, and R.E. Rockwood was a professor at Ohio State University. As early as 1904 groups of older boys at Camp Minocqua had experimented with canoe trips in the Canadian wilderness. By 1914, Dr. Sprague felt it was time to establish a base camp in Canada to expand the canoe exploration side of the Minocqua operation. A site was found on Baril Lake and in 1914 Camp Windigo was formed to provide a home base.

Little more than an elementary collection of tent platforms. Camp Windigo was set up for groups of thirty boys and men ranging in age from 15 to 60 who all had previous Minocqua experience. One of the guides who had actually been on Baril Lake at the time of the Dawson Trail was a man known as "Old Joe". Camp Windigo did not survive long. By 1918, or thereabouts, it had been closed. It is possible that America's entry into World War I had something to do with the camp's end.

DUKE CHILDS

At the end of World War I there were very few private camps for youth in either the United States or Canada. Those that were successful could probably be counted on one hand, and included the Kewadin Camps and some of the early western camps, such as the Cheley Camps in Colorado. The camping movement did not really flourish until many years later, when many private "wilderness" and special interest (horseback, hockey, swimming etc.) camps were started. However, in 1919 Wilfred L. Childs, "Duke" to most who knew him, decided the time was appropriate to find a suitable site for a permanent summer camp.

Duke Childs was a man whose life was dedicated to boys. He was an athletic coach, teacher and lover of the wilderness. He believed deeply in the benefits that came to those who, like Nessmuk and perhaps Thoreau, had experienced a close relationship with nature and the outdoor life while growing up. Thoreau said,

> *"I went to live in the woods because I wished to live*
> *deliberately, to front only the essential facts of life, and see*
> *if I could not learn what it had to teach, and not, when I*
> *came to die, to discover that I had not lived..."*

Childs attended the University of Chicago during its earliest years, and served as an assistant coach under the legendary Amos Alonzo Stagg. He coached basketball and gymnastics three years, bringing to the University its first conference championship in basketball. His decision to become a teacher himself was made at this time. After his graduation from Chicago (he had also studied at Harvard and Yale), he was offered a position in Winnetka, Illinois at the recently established New Trier Township High School. In 1909 he joined the faculty of New Trier and remained until his retirement in 1956. During his tenure at New Trier he coached, at one time or another, virtually every sport offered in the curriculum, including baseball, football, basketball, track, gymnastics, as well as conducting regular classes in Physical Education.

Teaching provided Childs the opportunity to pursue his dream of establishing a wilderness camp for boys during the summer vacation period. His own direct experiences with camping began with his directorship of a YMCA camp for 100 boys in 1907, and for the next twelve years he was affiliated with a number of private camps. Meanwhile, he embarked on an extensive search to find the perfect place to start a camp of his own. The camp site had to be reasonably near metropolitan areas from where the campers would come, mostly from the midwest. The Chicago area, and Minneapolis - St. Paul were considerations initially; many of the early campers came from these cities. Wisconsin, with its many lakes, seemed to be a likely possibility, for, with more roads being built in the northern part of the state, it was then possible to drive to some of the more remote lakes.

There were drawbacks, however. Most of the waterfront land had been placed in private ownership, and as such was not available. There were also limitations on the water routes for canoe trips; Childs had already decided that the new camp would be primarily a canoe trip operation. Wisconsin, and Minnesota as well, were ruled out as possible locations for the camp. Wilderness in 1919 meant only one of two directions; either westward or northward. West was out of the question because of the long travel distances required, so north was the primary option left after the elimination of Wisconsin and Minnesota. North meant Canada, and specifically Ontario.

When Duke planned the camp, he concluded that the best plan was to structure the operation around canoe trips as the fundamental way to experience the natural benefits of the wilderness he felt were so important. On the other hand, recognizing as he did, the values of the development of athletic skills of boys, and, with them, the aspect of competition (an important factor in that day and age), he would have to be sure that the new camp had enough physical space on which to build a variety of facilities.

In 1919 Childs and a canoe party consisting of a few experienced canoeists and several other husky teenagers set out to explore the wilderness of northern Ontario to find a place to establish a camp. They started in the watershed of Rainy Lake, actually in the newly-established Quetico Provincial Park, which had been chartered in 1912. They traveled generally northward until they reached the northern borders of the Quetico, and then both westward and eastward. To the west the lakes were big, and potentially dangerous to novice canoeists. Rainy Lake and The Lake of The Woods are two such examples. Still, the entire area seemed fruitful for canoe routes, for this had been the region that the Northwest Company and the Hudson's Bay company had once traversed during the fur trading era. Traders from these companies traveled by canoe from the lakehead (now Thunder Bay) near the Grand Portage on Lake Superior, through the lake country as far as possible in search of furs to be traded from the Indians. There were usable canoe routes with connecting portages between the lakes for Childs and his party to follow.

Duke's explorations eventually turned to the east, away from the big lakes, and worked their way somewhat northward. The northern boundary of the Quetico Park was the right-of-way of the Canadian National Railroad. This was the south branch of the CNR, and ran from Fort William - Port Arthur (re-named Thunder Bay in the 1960's) on Lake Superior via Fort Frances to the west and finally reached Winnipeg, Manitoba. A more northern route of the CNR ran from the Thunder Bay via Sioux Lookout, and eventually to Winnipeg. At this time there were virtually no roads that penetrated this part of northwestern Ontario, and the only means of transportation were the existing railroads. The southern route of the CNR seemed to lie in the area that offered the most advantages to Childs, including the fact that it bordered the Quetico Park itself, with its hundreds of miles of mapped canoe trip routes and portages.

Eventually the exploration group probed the area north of the southern CNR line and moved gradually to the east. They traveled through Lac Des Mille Lacs, a large lake with many islands. At the west end of this lake was a portage that crossed into Baril Lake. It was upon this lake that Duke found his ideal location for his camp. Two of the islands on the lake seemed to be precisely what was needed. At the west end of Baril Lake was the Brule Portage, which connected Baril Lake to smaller Brule Lake to the west and south. Importantly, this portage crossed the CNR railroad tracks. The railroad milepost showed Mile 101, which meant that it was 101 miles west of the Canadian Lakehead at Fort William.

The two islands that Duke considered for the camp were very close together, with the larger of the two being separated from the mainland on the north shore of Baril Lake by a very narrow water channel. The larger island possessed an excellent natural harbor offering protection from the prevailing westerly winds. On the smaller island, which would later be connected by a bridge to the larger island, there were the remains of a simple log building. There were also remains of a couple of older, long abandoned log structures on the larger island. The building on the small island was the old Camp Windigo "clubhouse".

Apparently Camp Windigo did not formally acquire title to the two islands, in terms of having the islands surveyed, and it seemed that the Windigo group only used the smaller of the two adjoining islands for their base camp. Duke Childs and his canoe party decided that no better place could be found on which to build the new camp. Virtually all surrounding land in the area, including the two islands that Duke wished to buy were deemed "Crown land", or land in the public domain. There was no private property along the railroad for many miles, save a few pieces surveyed into townships, although none of them had been built upon between Fort William to Fort Frances. The only exceptions were at railroad section points usually close to twenty miles apart from one another. "Section gangs", personnel responsible for track and telegraph communication, lived at these points; perhaps only three or four people per section.

The land that Duke wanted to buy had to be surveyed. Phillips and Benner, a land survey firm did the necessary surveying. Payment was made to the Canadian government, and construction of Camp Owakonze was started.

The name Owakonze, originally appearing as O-Wa-Kon-Ze, is taken from the Chippewa or Ojibwa meaning "Determination". This name proved to be a fitting one for an undertaking which took a large vision and an enormous amount of determination to create, build and grow into something magnificent.

BUILDING OWAKONZE

Making the island sites (a total of 32 acres on the two islands) into a viable facility required massive efforts on the part of all those who became Owakonze's first "summer settlers". Although there had been the two or three old log buildings on the islands, the land was heavily overgrown and much clearing had to be started immediately. This operation, as well as many other early projects, took many years to complete, so the growth pattern of the physical camp was an ongoing process throughout its existence.

Childs was an unusual combination of practical realist and blue-sky dreamer, with probably more of the latter than the former. There was little he thought could not be done. This second characteristic of the man was repeatedly demonstrated during the years the camp operated. As a coach and teacher, Duke held the belief that every boy should be exposed to organized, well-planned, expert instruction in a wide number of differing physical activities. It was expected that all boys would participate in such activities whether or not they wished to do so. Following a period of instruction, there was an equally valuable component, which was active competition in the areas where instruction had been provided. Duke believed that a boy could not be expected to know whether or not he really enjoyed a certain activity until he had advanced beyond the "dub" stage. In view of this idea, therefore, it followed that a wide number of physical facilities would need to be constructed to make the camp what Childs felt it ought to be.

First among these facilities to be constructed was a baseball field/playing area. In some places this would not seem a monumental task, but in the wilds of northern Ontario, with nothing but human muscle-power to carve a flat level field out of a rocky island, it was truly remarkable that it was done. The project was started as early as 1920. Dynamite was used to blast away a hillside. A large area on the island, which had in fact been a bay, was laboriously filled by hand, using wheelbarrows and shovels of dirt blasted from the hillside. These efforts were somewhat supplemented later by a horse of doubtful age and disposition named Dan. Naturally, a stable needed to be built for Dan, which was another of the early structures. After Dan's demise, Maude took his place, and after her demise the stable became the camp's rifle range. Maude was, in turn, aided by the first mechanized equipment to be used at Owakonze, a 1919 model "Cletrac", an abbreviation for Cleveland Tractor, which burned gasoline at first, and later kerosene. The Cletrac survived until the recent present when it was finally retired from service as being a lethal weapon in the hands of an untrained operator; the machine had a habit of kicking back when being cranked (a good way to get teeth knocked out!), as well as spinning around 360 degrees and going the opposite direction with little warning. In the 1960s it was painted bright red with white spots on it and was named "The Icky". At length, the land clearing revealed a recognizable baseball field which began to be used for that purpose in 1922 or 1923. Every boy who had been a camper during those early years at Owakonze would contend that it was he, himself, personally, who built the ballfield; and it was almost true!

Duke's master plan for Owakonze was to provide for three age groups of boys which he divided into three separate camp units; Junior, Middler and Senior Camps. Each group would live on its own portion of the large island, separated from the others. There would be separate staff for each camp, and the three camps would have their own swimming dock. All campers and staff would come together at mealtimes, to eat in a large dining hall. Each camper would take a turn at setting, waiting on and clearing tables. They were also, at times, assigned to "work" committees to help with specific projects building, clearing land, cleaning up etc. These projects were for the benefit of the entire camp.

The first summer campers lived in tents erected on wooden platforms. It is probable that the tents were acquired as World War I army surplus. Early photos show these in detail. At first they were placed around the perimeter of the new ballfield and were later moved to more secluded locations on the island. The tents were soon replaced by wooden frame cabins. Building simple living accommodations is not a major problem in most places, but, in the bush, everything needed from nails and roofing paper to lumber and tools had to be brought in from the suppliers at Thunder Bay some 100 miles to the east. In the beginning, there was no train stop, or unloading platform on the CNR. Dickering with the CNR resulted in the railroad declaring that Milepost 101 would subsequently be known as Owakonze, and a simple station shelter was eventually erected with a baggage room at one end and a caboose-type railroad stove to provide heat when needed. Owakonze was always a flag stop and was shown on timetables. A green and white flag was waved when it was necessary to stop the train. The engineer would blow his whistle twice to acknowledge that he had seen the flag when he rounded the curve before the station.

Once materials were unloaded from the train they had to be transported across the Brule portage by hand, about a quarter-mile in length from the railroad track to Baril Lake, and then taken six miles down the lake to the camp islands. A large flat-bottomed barge was built and was towed by one of the earliest pieces of mechanical equipment on the lake; an outboard motor and boat. The motor itself survived until the early 1990's, and had on its fuel tank the inscription cast into the metal, "made by Ole Evinrude". As time went on, and construction increased, it was obvious that something else mechanical would be needed to haul things across Brule Portage, which at the time was nothing other than a footpath through the woods.

The footpath had to be made into an elemental road in order to haul increasingly heavy and frequent loads from the railroad to the lake. Several summers of intensive effort, including the use of dynamite and the Cletrac, which was brought to the portage on the barge, produced a usable, albeit hair-raising, road. In 1929 "Ditsie" arrived. Ditsie was a 1929 Model A Ford truck, purchased in Chicago, dismantled, shipped in pieces to Fort Frances, Ontario, put on the CNR and sent to Owakonze where it was re-assembled and placed into immediate service. It did yeoman duty from 1929 until it was honorably retired in the 1970's. For many years Ditsie hauled absolutely everything over the portage, from pianos to fuel drums, lumber, firewood, tons of food and everything else necessary to run a camp. Ditsie did not use the original metal frame, which soon would have been broken on the rough road, but instead used a wooden frame constructed at camp. The wooden frame allowed Ditsie to bend nicely around all the rocks and boulder outcroppings on the road. Ditsie had her share of experiences, as had the "Cletrac", repeatedly falling into the lake, having to be salvaged, raised, dried out and put back together again to run and haul more loads over the portage.

Living cabins were eventually completed and the tents were retired. Meanwhile, the large dining room was built. The original dining hall was a unique building, erected partially on a cantilever system over the water itself, with a large porch, or verandah, along two sides. On the harbor side was the "trip dock", where canoes would assemble for departure on canoe trips. Next to this was the "trip room", where all the necessities for canoe trips were kept; food, cooking gear, "wannigans", which were wooden boxes to contain supplies and on which the man in the middle of the canoe sat. The camp post office and general office were located in the dining hall. Mrs. Childs, known to all as "The Duchess", presided over both the post office and the camp office. Just outside the dining hall was the icehouse, and places for washing up before meals. The drinking water supply flowed through pipes in the icehouse and was always ice cold. Hot water for the kitchen and laundry (located in another facility) was heated by the wood-burning stoves. A mid-winter tragedy occurred in 1941 when this splendid building, including the ice house, was completely destroyed by fire. Prior to the 1942 camp season, a brand new dining hall and kitchen were hastily constructed, so the camp continued without interruption. The new facility lacked the charm of the old building, but was, and still is, perfectly functional.

Another of the first buildings to be constructed was a photographic darkroom. Boys were taught to not only take pictures, but to develop, print, and enlarge them. Duke had the work crew build a photo studio as early as 1922 or 1923. The building still stands and could still be used for its original purpose. A skilled photographer was on the camp staff.

The camp was an operating reality, and needed facilities were being built at a great rate. Cabins were erected to accommodate the staffmen who were married and permitted to bring their wives to camp. At the far end of the big island, away from the rest of the camp, was the "guest camp"; it was built for families and visitors to the camp, usually parents of campers. Sometimes a group of fathers would come to spend a week of fishing, with guides and equipment provided by the camp. In later years, visitors sometimes preferred to fly into camp by float plane, either from Fort Francis or from Fort William, although this was always expensive and seldom done. In emergencies, however, an airplane could be flown in quite quickly to transport persons needing medical treatment, or fighting forest fires. A camp hospital was built and housed the resident physician and his family. The camp always had a physician on it's staff. For a long time these doctors came from the University of Chicago, and later from the University of Kansas Medical Center.

Duke thought boys should learn to play tennis. No one had ever considered the "bush" of northern Ontario to be a suitable place for the construction of a tennis court. As was typical, this in no way deterred Duke from making not one, but two tennis courts, on either side of the ballfield. Once again a supreme effort was needed, especially since Duke decided that these were to be clay courts. First the land was further leveled, graded, by hand, and made ready for the clay. The trouble was there was no clay on the island. After the 1941 fire in the dining hall, clay was discovered, but not as early as the 1920's. The first clay had to be hauled from the far west end of the lake, by bargeload, pulled by the outboard motor and moved ashore in wheelbarrows. Naturally, it was necessary to build suitable tennis court backstops of wire, and benches to sit during instruction periods. Duke got it all done.

Much more mechanical equipment was found to be necessary as Owakonze's operation grew. A power house was needed, and as far back as the 1920's, essential electricity was provided by a generator. The original generator was replaced by a then-new Kohler generator in 1928 and more electric lighting was installed in the kitchen, dining hall, and shop areas to run the power tools. Near the power house there was a "carpenter's shack" for the many kinds of woodworking tools the camp now had on hand. Shortly, also in the 1920's, a large boathouse was built in the harbor, out over the water. By then the camp had acquired several power boats which needed to be housed.

Duke Childs knew that a true wilderness camping experience would require trained leaders, and thoroughly responsible adults to lead the canoe trips, some of which might be out of the camp setting for several weeks or more. He realized that the Owakonze staff was one of its most important assets. The camping season was a full eight weeks in length, starting immediately after the school year ended in June and ending just before the fall school term began. For the most part, most of the senior staff men were school teachers and coaches, most with wilderness experience. They were assisted by junior staffmen who were generally college upperclassmen, frequently studying to become teachers, who were often former Owakonze campers. This nucleus of trained staff personnel commonly returned to Owakonze year after year, thus assuring a solid background of wilderness experience and canoe guiding. It was one of Childs' habits to employ persons who had very special skills. In time, Owakonze boasted a four-oar racing shell, built in Seattle by the Pocock company, and shipped by rail from there to Owakonze. Duke had, on staff, a trained rowing crew man who needed a shell to practice his art and teach to campers. Another example of training was Duke's gymnastics staff. The gymnastics coach had been on the US Olympic team and was the gymnastics coach at New Trier High School. Owakonze had one of the world's first trampolines back in the 1920's. Duke built it at ground level, over an open pit with padding on the sides. It was removed in the 1970's, but not before countless boys heard, "Hey, hey, hey!! No jumping on the tramp when it's wet!" Ervin C. Gerber's, "Gerb", a loyal staffman for decades, voice rang loud and clear demanding instant compliance.

A swimming dock was built off the small island, and a swimming instructor who was a coach from Milwaukee was hired. "Gerb" was hired in 1929 and remained on the staff until the 1970's. In addition to swimming, Gerb was very interested in Canadian history and knew a great deal about the days of the fur trade and the Baril Lake area's involvement in it. His stories were fascinating to the campers. He was also passionately interested in nature and the flora and fauna of the area. In addition, he handled the camp's popular riflery program with great enthusiasm and distinction, as well as leading the community singing in the dining hall at mealtimes. Many will never forget the "Robert

Shaw Corale" and the rousing renditions of the *Wiffenpoof Song*, a myriad of college fight songs and *The Tavern In the Town*.

SPORTS AND ACTIVITIES

Water sports including aquaplaning, were popular during the early summers. The fastest motor boat available was used; later water skiing was included. Water baseball was popular in the 1920's. A unique innovation at Owakonze, and one which maintained an extremely high degree of popularity for several decades, was the camp's water slide. Invented by a company in Minnesota during the 1920's, this was a device that was meant to be built over the water using a wooden track with sleds on which wheels were mounted. The rider would mount the sled from a platform at the top of the track, then would shoot down, as one does on a coaster sled in the snow, out into the water some distance at the bottom, maintaining a high rate of speed during the descent and making a tremendous splash. Duke's water slide was different in one major detail: instead of being mounted over the water, the slide began high on top of a rocky cliff covered with pine trees near the senior camp cabins. The campers shot downhill between the trees, which had the effect of exaggerating the speed. It was built on high wooden trestles, in effect to raise the height of drop even more. It was exciting (and scary!) and a sure-fire way to go into the lake for a morning dip; there was no turning back!

Still another example of program development was the addition to the camp fleet of several C-boats, bilgeboard scows which were among the fastest type of sailboat in the world. These were popular on the lakes of Wisconsin and Minnesota where they were built. In addition to the C-boats, two catboats were added. Sailing regattas were held at intervals throughout the summer for the embryonic skippers, following a typical triangular course. Trophies were awarded at the final banquet at the end of the summer to the winning sailors; this, again, to exemplify the competitive aspect of activities so important to Duke. And just as sailing regattas honored the winning skippers, so were canoe regattas for the paddlers, and swimming meets for swimmers.

Two more sports of a comparatively minor nature were popular: one was bait casting and the other was horseshoes. Casting with hooks was not allowed for obvious reasons, so a series of casting rings made from painted copper pipe each painted a different color were made and floated off the trip dock. Each ring was worth different points; points were awarded for casting the entire circuit and landing a plug within the ring. Rings at a greater distance counted more. A line of horseshoe pits was constructed on the small island, near a flat area which had been filled in from the lake and was used in later years as a canoe dock. Horseshoe tournaments were regularly held and one staffman, a teacher from Evanston (Illinois) High School, was an excellent pitcher and became the "coach" for this activity.

Another popular activity, especially around mealtimes, was the tightrope. The tightrope was a heavy steel bar some thirty feet long, and strung about one foot above the ground between two posts. It was more difficult than it looked! Other activities near the

11

dining hall were a draw as the smells coming from the kitchen attracted campers long before the bell rang for meals. A couple of tetherball poles were erected next to the dining hall and were in constant use; after a rain the puddles made the tetherball competitions that much more interesting.

The dinnerbell was a large brass bell from a CNR locomotive, donated to the camp by the railroad. It was, and still (in 1996) is, mounted against the wall of the dining hall high atop a huge pole cut from a spruce tree. (There are several interesting accounts of having to replace the pole in subsequent years). The bell can be heard all over the island and was used to signal time changes for activities during the day, for call to quarters in the evening, for "taps" or lights out in the evening, as well as for wake-up in the morning. An occasional prankster would climb the bell pole and wrap a sock around the clapper so the bell would not ring.

Duke felt it was necessary to provide an indoor play area on the small island for use during inclement weather. The small island was now connected by a foot bridge to the large island, and became the site for one of the most remarkable buildings ever planned and executed by Childs. It was begun in 1937 and took two years to complete. This building had no interior roof bracing. Childs was an avid and expert badminton player, and he insisted that no overhead obstructions be in place which would deflect the shuttlecocks. A particular and patented roof design seemed to offer the best arrangement, but the roof's designer, when consulted, indicated that a heavy winter snow load would jeopardize the safety of the roof. Typically, Duke went ahead and built this "clubhouse", as it called to this day, but he did add flying buttresses outside the building to make more bracing for the exterior walls which were built from huge virgin Norway and white pine logs. Logs like those can no longer be found in today's forests; they have all been harvested for lumber. The clubhouse has a theatrical stage at one end for camp show productions, which were an integral part of the summer activities, and later a wrestling room and weight training area was added to the other end. The stage has a huge fieldstone fireplace for evening ceremonies of various types. This is, in truth, a remarkable building and since 1937 the roof has suffered no snow damage.

Although emphasis at Owakonze was always primarily on the athletic aspect of the development of the adolescent boy, there was another very important feature of the camp program which merits high praise and inclusion. Early in the staffing for Owakonze, Duke became acquainted with a highly unusual, talented and sophisticated gentleman whose name was William Reich. Bill Reich joined the Owakonze team in 1923 and became the camp's assistant director. He was a teacher in the Chicago school system, and was a very talented musician who wrote, arranged and played with skill. Although his primary instrument was the piano, which he played weekly on Chicago radio broadcast stations, he also played many other instruments equally well. He brought to Owakonze a gift of attracting campers and staging musical and dramatic productions. At first, when minstrel shows were popular, the camp put on a minstrel show during the final days of the camp season. At one point, Duke had bought the entire University of Chicago band instrument collection when the U. of C. quit big ten football... not only the instruments, but sheet music and all the band musicians' uniforms! Bill Reich would gather together all the campers who showed any musical aptitude at all, (and some who did not!) and form a stage band, which would then perform during the celebrations at the summer's end, including the banquet and final camp show. He rehearsed his band and orchestra in between the other activities. In addition, Bill presided at mealtimes on the piano for community singing, as well as for the Sunday services held on the small island on the rocks behind the clubhouse. Don Ickes took over these important functions as the years passed on.

Construction of more and more sophisticated physical facilities continued. Noteworthy among these was the building of a superb outdoor basketball floor, lined off with badminton courts, to replace a simpler one built in the earlier years. This floor was, at one time, termed one of the finest floors in all of Canada. It's full completion was halted by the onset of World War II, when building materials became impossible to obtain. Slated to be build as part of this structure at one end was an indoor rifle range to replace the one which had formerly been Maude's barn, but the indoor range was never finished. It was also apparent by the 1950's that more indoor space was needed during extended periods of rain when everyone was in camp. A large building was erected, housing the camp library, a number of ping pong tables and other indoor games. A full-length screened porch is on one side of the building, and the camp store occupied one corner. There were lots of Mackintosh toffee bars sold there! This building was built in 1957 and named Anderson Hall, after Carl and Ethyl Anderson, the long-time caretakers.

As the years progressed and the camp population became larger, it became apparent that, during the summer, the island seemed to get smaller and smaller, especially when the entire camp was in residence and not out on canoe trips. There was virtually no place where a staffman could get away and relax, read, write a Sunday sermon or plan a canoe trip, or just sleep. This problem was solved beautifully by the building of the Steven W. Kurtz Memorial Retreat. Steve Kurtz was an Owakonze camper, and later staffman who was killed in an automobile accident. His father Bill, known to some as The Big Half, had been a camper in the early 1920's. He and his wife, Mary, had visited camp in the early 1960's when Jim, Steve's younger brother, was a camper. When Steve died they wished to do something to memorialize him; they felt that he had spent the best years of his life at Owakonze. Accordingly, they donated funds to construct an A-Frame building atop a high rocky cliff overlooking the harbor and the lake. It was a good distance away from the rest of the camp activities. It was equipped with a conical wood-burning fireplace and later the kitchen was provided with a cook stove and refrigerator. It has two bedrooms, and was furnished with comfortable furniture. The Retreat was completed in 1966 and has been used extensively. A plaque was carved by Lee Schilleriff, one of the staffwives, who was a sculptor, with Steve's name and placed on a rock cairn outside the building.

CANOE TRIPS

The principle on which the canoe trips operated was essentially a simple one: the boys were to be out of camp on canoe trips about half of the time they were at Owakonze, and the other half in camp. In this way, each boy would have an ample opportunity to have individual coaching and instruction in the widest possible selection of activities, and with half of the camper group out on canoe trips, would be able to make the maximum use of the camp facilities. Each canoe trip was organized around three basic objectives: one would be an exploring trip which would attempt to go into new areas, where, perhaps, no canoe party had been before; a second type would take a circle trip which would start from Owakonze and return via a different route. The third type of trip might be what was termed a "highball" trip, which would have as its objective a distant destination and returning within a given time, possibly down through Quetico Park to Ely, Minnesota and back to camp in ten days of paddling or less. Usually nine boys would be assigned to each trip, and two or more staffmen, depending on the age of the campers; younger boys had more staff and supervision than older, more experienced canoe trippers. Boys, generally, were able to choose the kind of trip they wanted, although some adjustments were made to assure a reasonable balance of strength and experience on each trip. Another popular type of canoe trip was the fishing trip. This trip would often start out later in the morning and camp earlier in the day to allow ample time for fishing.

Each boy in camp, whether he be in the Junior, Middler, or Senior camp, was scheduled to go on three canoe trips during the summer. First trips would be somewhat shorter and provide break-in experiences, including things like pitching tents, camp cookery, fishing skills, making everyone comfortable in the woods in all kinds of weather, etc. The next two trips would be progressively longer, and depending on the age of the boys, would range from six to fourteen or more days, but each was in and of itself a challenging experience for the individual. The canoe trips were sent off in grand style following breakfast. In early years Bill Reich would serenade the trips with his cornet; Don Ickes took over the tradition by playing his accordion down on the trip dock.

Returning to the main camp following trips was, of course, a highlight of the summer. Each trip was heralded by the ringing of the bell to announce their arrival. There was the mandatory singing of the "trip song" composed during the current trip; the songs usually reflected the adventures that had happened on that particular trip. After singing their song, the canoeists were rewarded with homemade cookies, chocolate chip or peanut butter, handed out by the camp cooks. Mail call was next, followed by a cleansing sauna and a brisk jump in the lake.

TRANSPORTATION

Transportation into Baril Lake has always been somewhat of a challenge, particularly in the very early years. Initially, most of the campers and staff came from the mid-West, Chicago, Milwaukee, Minneapolis and points in between. The first travel arrangements provided for transporting the camp group from Chicago and intervening points, to Duluth, Minnesota at the west end of Lake Superior by railroad. There arrangements were made to embark upon a Great Lakes cruise ship, which then made an overnight passage to Fort William/Port Arthur (later Thunder Bay, and commonly called The Lakehead), on the north shore of the lake. From there the CNR took the entire camp group the final 101 miles to Owakonze, which, by now, was a whistle stop. The group would then walk across the portage and be hauled down the lake on the barge and in boats.

When rail service was extended from Duluth to International Falls, Minnesota and the cruise boats were no longer in service, transportation became somewhat simpler. An entire railroad train on the Chicago and Northwestern line was chartered by the camp, complete with baggage car, Pullman sleepers, dining car, and an observation car. It was pulled by a steam locomotive. The train would depart the main CNR station in Chicago in the early evening, pick up passengers along the north shore of Lake Michigan in many of the Chicago suburbs, Milwaukee and through Madison, Wisconsin and Duluth. The boys went to bed in assigned berths which were ready for them. The following morning they would have breakfast before reaching Duluth. The train had an entire day layover in Duluth before proceeding onward to International Falls that evening. The camp would reserve a suite of rooms at the Hotel Spaulding for the day which served as headquarters, and provided a noon meal in the hotel dining room. The boys spent the day exploring the city with staffmen accompanying the younger ones. Movies were the big attraction! After dinner in the hotel, the train was reboarded.

At this time Chicago Northwestern locomotives were only permitted to pull trains north as far as the US/Canadian border, and not into Canada, so the Canadian National Railroad would send a locomotive and tender all the way from Winnipeg, Manitoba to Duluth, where it was coupled to the Northwestern cars. The CNR also provided two railroad personnel to accompany the camp train; a traveling passenger agent and a traveling baggage agent to assist the group in crossing the international border at Fort Francis. The train departed Duluth in the early evening and traveled through the night, arriving at the border sometime after midnight. The on-board agent and customs/immigration men cleared the group and its baggage from the US into Canada without having to wake the campers or open their baggage. It was a very convenient and welcome arrangement by the CNR. The following morning, after breakfast in the dining car, the train arrived at Milepost 101, Owakonze. Ditsie would be at the train station and would be loaded with all the trunks and duffels. Everyone would walk the quarter-mile portage and ride the barge to the camp island. The baggage would be brought on a second barge load. At the end of the summer the entire process and travel would be reversed. This method of transportation lasted from about 1926 until the 1950's by which time the Chicago to Duluth service on the CNR was abandoned, and from Duluth to International Falls as well. The CNR, similarly, had reduced its schedule connecting Fort Frances, Ontario to Fort William. Major changes needed to be made.

The first major change in the transportation system occurred in the early 1950's and involved the charter of a DC-4 airliner to take the main group from Chicago to International Falls, Minnesota. Campers from other parts of the country would get to Chicago and meet the group there. At International Falls, means had to be found to transport the entire group with all of their baggage the final few miles across the international border to the CNR depot at Fort Frances, Ontario. Although CRN rail service had been drastically curtailed by then, there were still a few day coach trains that made the run from Winnipeg, via Fort Frances to Fort William. In order to move the group, as well as all the duffels, trunks, fishing poles, paddles etc., from the airport on the US side to the railroad depot on the Canadian side, school buses were hired to make the short run. The all-coach train then made the final lap to Owakonze. The airline charter was not the final transportation hurdle during the last years of the camp's operation. DC-4 aircraft went out of service when the larger DC-6 planes came along. However, the runways at the International Falls airport were not long enough to land the larger aircraft. It was time to get creative again with travel plans.

In 1943 the Steeprock iron mines in Atikokan, Ontario, approximately 80 miles east of International Falls, began to move ore from the town by railroad. In 1941 there were perhaps 100 people living in Atikokan; by 1943 the it had grown during the boom years to as many as 7000 people. At this time there was no road between Fort William and International Falls; the only method of transportation was the CNR which had a propensity to go out on strike at any time. Another means was needed to provide the necessities of life for the people of Atikokan when the train was on strike. During the strikes all the communities along the line, including Owakonze missed deliveries of food, mail, express and passenger service. In 1954 a road was constructed which ran from Fort William to Atikokan. Later this road, Highway 11, was extended from Atikokan to Fort Frances.

There was always logging being done after the new highway was finished, somewhat to the consternation of the people from Owakonze who found that their canoe routes and portages were frequently interfered with by logging operations. The logging did, however, have one major benefit that stood the camp in good stead from the late 1950's to the present day. In order to reach the interior areas which were to be logged, roads had to be cut into the bush from the Atikokan highway. These were nothing more than dirt surfaces, sometimes graveled; they were ungraded, full of stumps, windfalls, rocks, boulder outcroppings and other hazards. Meant for large logging trucks they were difficult and sometimes impossible to navigate.

One of these roads crossed Windigoostigwan Lake, a large lake west of Baril, about 16 miles distant from the camp. In the 1970's this road became the camp's principal access for personnel because the only remaining passenger service on the CNR was a single car train, known as a Budd car. This train carried perhaps 30 passengers and a crew of one motorman; no freight and little else. At first it did take the mail, but finally gave that up as well because the mail contract had been given to the trucking industry and was carried by truck. The camp lost its post office, and mail sent from Owakonze on the Budd car had to be disguised as "fish", in a prominently labeled box. It was sent down the line for proper mailing closer to civilization. This cooperative subterfuge permitted the camp to send and receive mail at irregular intervals.

Once train travel from the Chicago area and points beyond was eliminated, including the CNR line, the only feasible alternative transportation of campers and staff seemed to be bus service. Three large transcontinental Greyhound buses were chartered in Chicago. Meal and rest stops were arranged for en route; the buses hauled everyone to Owakonze via Duluth and Fort Frances. Taking Greyhound buses down the Windigoostigwan road was no easy task! The road was about 8 miles long, narrow, steep and rocky. The buses managed to not only drive down and discharge the passengers, but were able to even turn around. This route saved the camp for several seasons!

Once at the bottom of the road the campers were still some 16 miles from the camp, which meant they had their baptism of canoeing immediately after getting off the buses. The entire camp body and staff members paddled down Lake Windigoostigwan through to Brule Creek and into Brule Lake to the portage connecting to Baril Lake in canoes which had been towed to the road. Staff wives and small children were ferried in small boats. At the portage, the wives and children were usually taken by Ditsie to the other side of the portage; all the rest walked. The luggage was brought in boats and by Ditsie over the portage as well. It was a *major* undertaking, which usually went off extremely well considering the difficulties of moving some 100 people in this manner. The entire process was reversed at the end of camp. All who were involved with the procedure prayed for calm days with no rain! For some it was a rough indoctrination to Owakonze, and was somewhat labor intensive, but it worked.

Getting supplies into camp after the CNR had shut down was another major problem. The problem was solved for a short time with the creation of yet another lumbering road; this time again crossing Windigoostigwan, but at the eastern end about 16 miles closer to Owakonze. Brule Creek and Brule Lake still had to be crossed, as well as Brule portage. The new lumber camp road crossed a bridge at the end of Brule Creek and was a much wider, graveled road, open to public access and was even somewhat graded. It was maintained as an all weather road by the Great Lakes Paper Company. This meant that trucks with supplies could be driven as far as the Brule Creek bridge, then were met by boats from camp. Goods would be loaded at the bridge and hauled up Brule Lake to the end of the portage and then by truck to the dock on Baril Lake. Many of the shipments were heavy loads; 45 gallon oil drums with gasoline, kerosene and oil, as well as lumber for building purposes, food, and propane cylinders that weighed one hundred pounds apiece. The camp stoves had been converted from using firewood to propane gas because of conservation issues dealing with the cutting of firewood. Propane was needed for the kitchen and laundry for the entire summer season. A sturdy workboat was left on Brule Lake for the purpose of hauling all the heavy goods.

The last chapter in the saga of camp logistics occurred after the logging road to the bridge was extended further to a point there it actually met the Baril Lake shoreline. For the first time in its history, Owakonze was directly accessible to the outside world by roadway. At first it was viewed with consternation because the true wilderness character of the area was threatened by a road to the lake. It soon became clear that without the road there was no way the camp could continue to survive. There was no other way either personnel or supplies could get in or out, except by bush plane which was prohibitively expensive, and dependent upon good weather.

It is obvious that the Canadian National Railroad played an integral part in the formative years of Owakonze. Indeed, there are literally hundreds of stories that have been told through the years chronicling the ups and downs, trials and travails of the CNR and all who were dependent upon it's service. Originally the passenger service ran twice a day so that it could be flagged down in the morning for a run into town and then taken back out the same evening. The passenger trains would carry some express packages, but express was far more expensive than freight rates, and some items, lumber, drums of oil and kerosene, and case lots of packaged foodstuff, could not be handled by express and had to sent on the "local". Every year the camp would arrange to have a especially large shipment brought in, consisting of most of the bulk foods for the season and whatever large lumber orders there were. An entire barge load of food came in as soon as there was a crew on hand to unload and transport it from the train to camp.

The "local" merits special mention for it was, in truth, a most unique railroad train. It had no discernible timetable, and left Fort William early in the morning to make its weekly run to Fort Frances, 200 miles west. It stopped everywhere it had something to either load or unload. Occasionally the train crew would stop the train and pick blueberries! When this happened, the entire line would come to a halt, because there was no central traffic control for the trains at that time. While the trainmen filled themselves with blueberries, the dispatcher in Fort William would be tearing his hair out because no train could move. At one time a mistake was made when the "local" was directed to dump a gondola car full of gravel at a certain place on a siding. The entire load was dumped at the wrong end of the siding, so it all had to be reloaded, at great expense of time and further distraction of the poor dispatcher. Once in a while an Owakonze canoe trip would need to travel a short distance on the railroad, when the water levels in rivers were low, or portages were blocked. They would wait for the "local", flag it down, load their canoes into an empty box car and tell the train crew what lake they wanted to stop at. Sometimes the train crew would simply forget where the lake was, and by the time the train could be stopped they were several miles from where they wanted to be. The train would simply back up until they got to the right lake and would not continue on until the canoeists were dropped at their destination. This service cost about three dollars per canoe, but much of the time the fee was never collected.

One particularly amusing incident happened about the time the railroad was switching to diesel locomotives from steam engines. Before the changeover was complete the dispatcher decided that the favorite engine the "local" had been using was larger than necessary for its weekly run. They assigned a smaller locomotive to the train, and the crew felt they had to do something to get their old engine back. The "local" left Fort Frances one morning and the plan went into effect. Every time the train came to even the slightest uphill grade the engineer would manage to make it appear that the engine was underpowered to climb the hill. They would set up the brakes, uncouple the front half of the train, leaving the rear half at a standstill on the main line, brakes locked while the engine hauled the front end up to the next siding. They repeated this exercise over and over again all the way to Fort William. The beleaguered dispatcher could do nothing except to wait each time; meanwhile all traffic on the south branch of the CNR stood still. The following week the "local" crew got their favorite engine back again. Eventually the "local" service was eliminated. This elimination caused serious problems for the camp in regards to shipping supplies. It is clear that it was largely due to the cessation of railroad service that caused the Camp Owakonze to close operations after 1973. Subsequently it was opened and run in different configurations for a few years and then was bought by Boy's Hope out of St. Louis, and continues to be run in the 1990's.

KITCHEN

Cooking was done on wood-burning lumber camp stoves from the 1920's until the 1960's. Hot water for dish washing and other kitchen use was provided by the same stove fires. Wood for the two stoves was stored in bins under the kitchen counters that were filled daily from outside the building. Once every summer the entire camp took part in carrying logs from the bush, both on the island and from the mainland. Logs were cut and trimmed by the caretaker and his assistants. Before chainsaws were common, the Cletrac was belted to a large circular saw and the logs were cut to stove length and poled near the kitchen to be split during the winter when wood splits more easily. This was always a major job for the caretaker who lived on the camp island year round.

Another task during wintertime was to keep the roofs clear of snow; an arduous job with many feet of snow to shovel off each building. In addition to snow removal, the caretaker also had to cut ice from the lake to pack in the icehouse. This operation necessitated keeping an area clear of snow so the ice would freeze as thick as possible. Ice was generally cut in February or March when is had reached some thirty inches thick. Ice harvesting required several days of hard work and it was usually necessary for the caretaker to bring in another man to help, although many years his wife, and or children, would assist. Originally, cuts were made in the ice with an ice saw; a large toothed saw much like an oversized carpenter's saw. Then, using ice tongs suspended from a tripod log structure with a movable boom and a heavy counterweight to balance the weight of the ice blocks, the blocks were removed from the lake. Each of the blocks weighed several hundred pounds. The boom swung around, depositing each block on an inclined track and slid up into the icehouse. The icehouse itself was built of logs with double walls. Sawdust was packed between the two walls providing an effective insulating blanket so the ice would last through the following summer. Another chore at the end of the summer was to remove the sawdust, pack it into burlap bags and air dry it for reuse the following year. The sawdust came from the wood sawing operation, as well as from any lumber camp operating in the area. The ice house was a magical haven for small children on hot summer days; playing in the moist, cold saw dust and blocks of ice. Constructing forts was wonderful! In later years the ice cutting was done with gasoline chainsaws which was much faster, but difficult because icy cold water was splashed all over the ice cutters.

More recently, two additions were made to the camp's refrigeration system. A metal-lined "cold room" was built to provide refrigerated storage for the cans of milk brought in by the railroad three times a week. The "cold room" also stored meats, which were suspended by hooks from the ceiling, as well as butter, fresh vegetables and other perishable foods. Ice from the adjacent ice house had to be continually repacked in the "cold room". The blocks were hosed off with water and repacked around the boxes and cans stored there. On Saturday nights the train would bring five gallons of ice cream for the Sunday noon meal. One of the headwaiter's jobs was to repack the ice cream into an old-fashioned freezer with rock salt and crushed ice and churn it until it was as hard as could be made.

As the number of people on the island increased, reaching some years to as many as 150 persons, it was felt necessary to create a "walk-in" refrigerator with refrigeration pipes and an electric motor to power its compressor. This cooler was always kept near zero degrees, which made it easier to store foods for longer periods. This was especially helpful after the CNR began to cut back on the frequency of the train service before finally abandoning it altogether.

COMMUNICATION

The camp had a post office from its earliest years. The Canadian postal service, through the District Director of Postal Service in Winnipeg, provided stamps, mailbags, and all the other necessary materials for what was known as a "summer post office". Mail was dispatched via CNR twice a week on the westbound train to Fort Frances, Ontario. The same train would bring the incoming mail from Fort William to the east. At the same time mail was handled other necessities were received - food, milk, express packages and the like. Mrs. Childs served for many years as the camp's postmistress. Her term was followed by Don Ickes, who proudly held the honor of being the only American who was an official Post Master.

In addition to regular mail service there were some rather unusual methods of communication during the years of camp operation. The first of these was a unique service provided by the CNR. There was only telegraph service during the early years along the railroad right-of-way; telephones were not available yet. The CNR constructed a railroad siding at Owakonze, brought in a freight caboose and switched it off the main line onto the siding. They arranged for a CNR telegrapher to be housed during the camp's summer season for the sole purpose of sending and receiving the camp's telegrams. Telegrams were sent either to Fort William or Fort Frances to suppliers for things to be sent on the railroad, either the regular run or the "local", or by the express passenger trains. At one time it was possible to go into town in the morning, conduct business and return to Owakonze the same night. Before the telegraph was in place, all telegrams had to be put on the train at Owakonze and sent to Fort William or Fort Frances to be sent on from there.

One telegrapher was a one-legged man who brought his entire family with him during his summer term. The caboose was fairly close to the main line track, and just at the end of a sharp curve, with a steep grade ahead. When the old steam locomotives came from the west, they poured on the coal to get up the grade, and the telegrapher, when he heard the whistle from the approaching train, would get his entire family out of bed. They climbed down the ladder stairs to the caboose and moved up the hill behind the siding to a safe distance as the train approached the curve, lest it come off the track and take the caboose with it. Some nights they must not have gotten much sleep because there was a lot of rail traffic in those early days!

Duke thought it would be easier to send telegrams if he could somehow telephone down to the railroad from the camp office. He embarked on another major operation: he had the work crew string a bare galvanized telephone wire from the camp office across the island and to the mainland, which was close behind the camp. From there it was necessary to string the wire alone the shoreline, following the curvature of Baril Lake, around every bay and inlet, until they finally got to the far west end and crossed the portage to the telegrapher and his caboose. It was about six miles as the crow flies between camp and the portage, but following the lake shore it was perhaps fifteen miles. The system worked -- more or less! The trouble was twofold: each time there was a bad storm, trees and limbs would fall across the line, breaking the wire, or a moose or deer would get his antlers snagged in the wire and drag it far back into the bush. Each time there was a break it meant that someone had to walk the entire line to find the broken wire and repair it. Eventually it was no longer sensible to keep it constantly in repair and the line was abandoned. It should be noted that despite all the known problems with stringing phone lines along the shore, Don Ickes undertook the same project and strung a phone line from the camp island down to 2-Mile Island in the 1960s! His children, under some duress, all spent time following the shore line looking for the breaks. Even though it was a hassle, having that phone line when Eleanor Ickes and her children were alone on 2-Mile Island was good for peace of mind; it served its purpose when the Ickes sailboat broke loose on a very windy day and Eleanor was able to call down to camp for help. Don would frequently call 2-Mile Island from camp where he was working and tell Eleanor to "bring some spikes down for dinner!".

In the early 1950's, the CNR began to use telephones along the line, so the telegrapher's duty was terminated. About the same time, block signals were installed to provide automatic traffic control and hopefully reduce the number of serious derailments and head-on collisions that occurred each summer. Also, heavier gauge rail was installed. The new iron mines in Atikokan, some 40 miles west of Owakonze, had further increased rail traffic and heavier loads were carried. There were still the regular package freight trains and grain trains carrying wheat from the prairies to Fort William to be loaded on ships on Lake Superior. Now there were also iron ore trains and the thrice weekly passenger trains. The railroad later installed a "dispatcher's" telephone in the station shed at Owakonze in a locked metal box for which the camp was given a key. Permission was granted to use this phone at times when no railroad traffic was being passed. The camp could now call the dispatcher and ask him where the train was, (meaning how late it was!). The dispatcher would give an answer if he was in an agreeable mood, and if he was not he would simply refuse to answer. Many people have "fond" memories of waiting interminably long times for the almost always late CNR. One of the favorite games invented during the waits was chucking rocks up into the chimney of the warming stove. By the end of the summer the stove would be quite full of rocks! Balancing on the rails and seeing how far one could walk on them with their eyes closed was another common pastime.

By about 1954 the Northern Telephone company had strung its lines to a point about six miles to the west of Owakonze, and the camp arranged to have this wire extended to a telephone near the Owakonze station, where a phone would be installed within a wooden box nailed to the pole. This was an extremely expensive project, because the camp had to pay the entire cost of extending the line the full six miles. Later still, in the 1960's, this line was further extended across the portage to the dock area at the end of Baril Lake, where a sort of emergency cabin had been built for the caretaker's use during freezeup in the fall and breakup of the ice in the spring.

There was a somewhat abortive attempt in the late 1950's to use a newly-invented radio telephone, but it proved unsatisfactory and was only in service a short time. Don Ickes was an amateur radio operator (radio "ham"), and for some years set up his equipment in the camp office and was able to send emergency messages when necessary. There were a number of cooperative radio hams in several parts of the United States and Canada who had regular "schedules" to pass information back and forth. The system worked quite well, but because of the "amateur" nature of the service, no messages of anything resembling a commercial nature could be sent or received, so it was not a true substitute for the telephone. However, a number of emergencies were resolved a lot more expediently with Don's ability to quickly contact float planes for evacuation. Don continued to use his radio to pass "traffic" (messages) and have schedules through his last summer visit to 2-Mile Island in the early 1990's.

The final chapter in the communications story came much later. A state-of-the-art radiotelephone is now in use at the camp, employing a high antenna structure and regular touch tone phones can be operated from storage batteries. It is now possible to call the camp directly from anywhere with regular telephone service. Having the phone there is a mixed blessing; it has brought the outside world a lot closer than many would like to have it, although the convenience cannot be denied.

CAMP OWAKONZE, LTD.

Duke Childs eventually reached the age of retirement from his teaching position and found it more difficult to continue his Owakonze interests with efficiency. He began to consider selling the camp properties around 1952. A group formed, consisting of a number of men who had been either Owakonze campers or staff members and had worked closely with Duke; indeed some were still active members of the staff, and some had their own sons then attending the camp. All firmly believed in the same values which had been held by Duke. A price was agreed upon and Camp Owakonze became Camp Owakonze LTD; a limited corporation owned by its alumni shareholders, or camp sponsors, as they were called. One of group, Peter A. Frantzen, had started at Owakonze as a staff member in 1937 and became its new Camp Director, and was placed on salary. The newly-organized camp continued under this structure until its final year of sponsorship operation in 1973.

Pete Frantzen had been a teacher and coach at New Trier Township High School and had worked closely with Duke Childs for many years. He served as Director of Owakonze until his own retirement from teaching. Frantzen was replaced by Harvey F. Dickinson, who served as athletic director at Hinsdale, Illinois Central High School, and enjoyed several summers of successful leadership at Owakonze. Dickinson was succeeded in turn by Jack Hays, who was on the athletic staff of Northern Illinois University at DeKalb, Illinois. After Jack Hays' departure, a young man who had grown up with Owakonze, first as a camper and later a valued staff member, Brian (Barney) Swett, was permitted to lease the camp under the supervision of the camp sponsors. Pete Frantzen agreed to return out of retirement to assist Barney. After two or three years it became obvious that the logistics problems of transportation and supply were simply too difficult to surmount, so 1973 became Owakonze's final operating season.

Several additional factors served to bring the original Owakonze to a close in 1973. One of these, certainly, was the continuing growth of summer school programs for high school age youths. Additionally, the competition from other kinds of camps, including the single-purpose camps (tennis camps, baseball camps etc.) became more intensive each year. Also, there was a growing trend for families to vacation together. Outdoor recreation assumed a different form by 1973 than it had in 1920! A number of things were tried to counteract these forces, all of which helped somewhat in the short run, but none had any long term effect.

One of these trials was a "split season". The campers could elect to spend the entire summer at Owakonze, or a half-summer, either the first or second half. The problem encountered was that a camper would sometimes enroll for the first session and then decide that he wanted to stay for the second, only to find that his family had made other plans and he had to go home whether he wanted to or not. Transportation arrangements were thus difficult to plan. Another experiment tried was a girls camp, which lasted with some success for several summers. High school girls were enrolled as a small group with their own staff, and were a carefully chosen group to provide a smooth integration into what was still essentially a boys camp. Many of the girls were sisters or friends of boys who had spent their summers at Owakonze. They followed their own canoe trip schedule and one or two men usually accompanied them to act as guides.

The sponsorship group still retained ownership of the camp properties and began attempts to sell the camp and all its assets. A potential ownership group whose members included John Mangel and Bob Drake, property owners on thelake and old Owanknze alumni, bought the camp, but never successfully ran it. They, in turn, sold it to another ex-camper and staffman, Frances Neir (Frannie) whose father, also Frances Neir, had been one of the earliest Owakonze campers in the 1920's. Frannie then sold Owakonze to a group called Boys Hope, who continue to run the camp at this time (1995). This organization functions within the Catholic church, and is based in St. Louis. Father Paul Sheridan served as director of Boys Hope until 1996. Through the program, residence houses have been made available for high school age boys who have experienced difficulty at home through abuse, neglect, or perhaps, have had no real home. They are cared for in Boys Hope's housing with staff guidance and educational counseling. One of Boys Hope's concepts is very similar, actually, to Duke Childs' beliefs: that all youths should learn to appreciate nature in a basic way through direct, purposeful experiences such as those that can be gained by spending their summers at a place in the wilderness like Owakonze.

Today, Boys Hope has prospered under the leadership of Paul Sheridan, and Owakonze has also not only survived the seemingly insurmountable obstacles it faced for some years, but has thrived. Though quite different from the Owakonze of earlier years, it continues as a boys camp, inculcating the same basic values it always did. From a small number of residence homes, Boys Hope has expanded to many such houses spread throughout the US and other countries. It has attracted prominent people to its board of directors and executive committees and actively engages in fund raising, which has meant that Owakonze, as an integral part of their program, is able to continue in a healthy and prosperous manner. Boys Hope quickly established is own traditions, some of which are very similar to the original camp, others of which reflect the type of program and boys that it serves. It is fervently hoped that Boys Hope will be able to continue to operate the camp successfully for many years to come.

ADVANCED TRIPS

By 1961, with Owakonze now under the leadership of its new group of sponsors, planning was begun for a new and heretofore untried approach to canoe tripping that was named "The Advanced Trip Program". The concept was to provide a special, long, and exciting canoe trip annually for those Owakonze campers who had excelled during the regular canoe trips taken as a part of the camp offering. Eight or nine boys and two staffmen generally made up the trip complement. Boys were to be carefully selected for the first of these trips which was scheduled for the 1962 camp season. It may be observed that there was a kind of similarity between Owakonze's new plan for the 1962 and Dr. Sprague's Windigo "outpost" program of 1912 for experienced campers from Minocqua, but the Owakonze plan was far more ambitious.

Planning for the advanced trips was generally begun as far ahead as one year. Routes were carefully considered, maps and topographical surveys were obtained, diaries of those who had taken the same trip were studied thoroughly, and the entire logistics involved with this kind of an operation were carefully worked out. Such details as supplies of food, transportation requirements, the type of equipment needed, division of loads to be carried, disposition of personnel canoe by canoe, staff supervision and safety issues all needed to be addressed. As campers were chosen for the trip, regular meetings were held throughout the off-season to plan in greater detail.

One of the camp sponsors, Frank B. Hubachek Jr. (Bill), was the spark plug for the original idea, and its driving force for many years. Hubachek and his father both had extensive woods experience in the Canadian lake country. Bill had been a camper at Owakonze under Duke starting in 1935. He was adamant in emphasizing the critical need for detailed planning, down to the smallest detail. Meetings of the camper group and staff were frequently held in his home. Where necessary, special equipment was procured for use on the advanced trips. Because many of the routes considered for the trips were in the sub-arctic, and one in the "high arctic", proper clothing, rain gear, tents, foot wear and insect protection had to be carefully researched and the best of what was available was obtained.

Between the years of 1962 and 1973 most of the advanced trips had Hudson's Bay as the final destination. This was, in part, due to the fact that there are many navigable rivers which flow into the Bay, the Albany and the Attawapiskat to name only two. In addition, many large lakes, such as Lake St. Joseph, make canoe travel for great distances possible.

In 1965, the trip started at Sioux Lookout, in northwestern Ontario, and traveled through Lake St. Joseph, and the Albany River to its end at James Bay, (a portion of Hudson's Bay). The Albany route combines good fishing, plenty of thrilling rapids, and interesting country with occasional Indian settlements and historic Hudson's Bay Company posts. From the mouth to the Albany the crew negotiated approximately 90 miles of tidal ocean paddling as they made their way down to Moosonee on the Moose River.

The first fifteen days of the trip were led by Bill Hubachek. At the fifteen day point, staffman Steve Kling, also a former Owakonze camper, was flown in by Geroge Mangle ("Magoo") , another former camper and staffman, to Miminiska on the Albany River to take over the leadership of the trip. They brought in mail and even some ice cream (!) from the Owakonze ice house. This entire trip lasted for 40 days.

The 1967 advanced trip was certainly the most extensive and enterprising of the entire program, before and after that year. The final destination of the trip was a tiny outpost on the far northeast shore of Hudson's Bay known as Baker Lake, which is about as far north as one can conveniently travel with only a few exceptions. The trippers went by rail with all of their gear from Owakonze to Yellowknife, in the Northwest Territories. From there, they launched their canoes at Artillery Lake, which in late June was still largely icebound. Paddling through loose pack ice, they found themselves in real Eskimo country, with caribou and musk oxen. The trip followed the Thelon River to Baker Lake, and then via Chesterfield Inlet to the shores of Hudson's Bay where they delighted in paddling amidst schools of small white whales. The last advanced trip took place in 1973 and also ended on Hudson's Bay, this time via the God's River and the Hayes River, and ended at York Factory.

CARETAKERS AND NEIGHBORS

The first camp caretaker was Rae Stout. The second was Carl Anderson who, with his wife Ethel, were caretaker and head cook for many years. Ethels's kitchen assistants included Phyllis Ljungqvist, Ella Lofgren and Adele Sundberg, who subsequently held the position of head cook in the 1960's and 1970's. The husbands of the cooking staff, Axel Ljungqvist and Eric Lofgren were employed as skilled carpenters, and all were Scandinavians.

Carl Anderson and Ethel, whose maiden name was Tillberg, were at Owakonze from the early 1950's until ill health forced Carl to move into Port Arthur in the 1960's. Ethel's brother, Pete Tillberg was one of the two or three master carpenters on Duke's staff at one time or another. It was Pete Tillberg who supervised the building of the Clubhouse in 1937; he also built the first really winter-proof caretakers house, made in the Swedish style using square-hewn logs mortised together at each end. It was two stories high, with indoor plumbing and running water (in the summer), and a simple basement; it was another marvelous example of woodsmanship and was in use as the caretakers house until 1994, when the current caretaker, Rene Kreis built a new house a few yards away.

Carl, Axel and Eric worked, frequently, as a team. Each seemed to know intuitively what the other wanted or needed. The difference was that Eric chatted like a magpie all of the time, and Axel, much more taciturn by nature, seldom said anything. Axel would admonish Eric by saying, "Eric, you talk too much!" Axel and Carl could both do things with an ax another person less skilled would need a shopsmith to duplicate. A regular Sunday job for both was sharpening their tools. When the new and enlarged boathouse was built in 1958, on the same site as the earlier boathouse, Carl and Axel sat together on a log and did some scratching on an old piece of masonite with a pencil. Then they went ahead and built a fine new boathouse, complete with three boat slips under a roof built with an elaborate truss system. When it was all finished, Carl was found scowling darkly and looking at his plan sketched on the shingle. He muttered about something being wrong, and, when pressed for details, he replied that the building "had been done wrong!". He took a measuring tape out and ran it out one side of the building from the shore to the outer end, and did the same thing at the opposite side. It turned out that one side was approximately four inches longer than the other! His eye was that accurate and he spotted the error immediately.

Axel was a gentle giant of a man who was adored by all the small children on the island. He was a superb wood carver. Every summer he would lovingly carve things for each of them; these works of folk art are still treasured. One summer he carved paddles for all the kids, each a different size, as befitting the size of the child, and on each one he varnished a cutout of the Donald Duck logo that came on the large cans of juice. Another summer Eric made a high chair for dolls complete with a tray that raised and lowered, as well as a doll cradle. Every year he would hand carve all the banquet favors for everyone on the island; one year they were miniature paddles, another a tiny wooden ax stuck in a log. He had always wanted to play the violin, but had never seen one up close. He found a good picture of one in the Eaton's catalog and made one that winter and then learned to play it. Axel's wife, Phyllis, was a delightful, jolly, round woman with white hair and a ruddy complexion. She was a wonderful cook and had the hidden talent of singing. Upon occasion she could be convinced to stand on the stage in the clubhouse during the Camp Show and sing *"The Biggest Aspidistra in the World"*, a song which all the children thought was titled, *"The Biggest Extra Ashtray in the World!"*.

Joe Kreis and his first wife, Bunnie Tenniscoe Kreis took over caretakership when Carl retired. Bunnie had been born and raised in the area; she was one of 19 or so children of Frank Tenniscoe and his wife, several of whom worked over the years for Owakonze as handy men, carpenters etc. Joe was a Luxumberger who emigrated to Canada after World War II. He had been captured and interned as a young man by the Germans who taught him to weld. Because he was a young and healthy man, his life was spared and he was made a member of the Hitler Youth. Upon arrival in Canada he ended up near Thunder Bay and went to work in a sawmill down the railroad from Owakonze. He became Carl's assistant for several years before Carl retired. Bunnie and Joe were divorced in the late 1960's, after their children, Rocky and Rene were of school age and were spending their school years in Atikokan. The seclusion and isolation, and the fact that her children were being boarded away from home was difficult for Bunnie. After several years of being single Joe married Delano LeValley ("Dink") in the later 1970's. Joe drowned in 1990, and his younger son, Rene, took over the duties of being Owakonze's caretaker.

When Joe first came to Owakonze he was a classic example of a "jack-of-all-trades". Eventually he became master of many, with a few notable exceptions, chief among which was his failure to comprehend electricity. The camp went through auto storage batteries like mad because Joe could not believe that batteries should not be stored on cement floors for extended periods of time. Batteries lose their charge when stored on cement. Joe's solution was simply to connect them to a battery charger and all would be well again. It was rather like mysteriously pouring the electricity back into the dead battery, like filling a pail of water. Still, he managed to do some noteworthy things using electricity, somehow without electrocuting himself in the process!

One day in the early 1960's, Joe announced that he was going to get himself a television set. He was an ardent ice hockey fan and wanted to be able to watch the games during the winter. Everyone told him that Owakonze, being 100 miles from the nearest television station, would never be able to receive a usable signal. Undeterred by such negative predictions, Joe went off to Atikokan and returned with an off-brand TV set, the manufacturer of which no one had ever heard. He bought an outside antenna which he erected on the roof of the woodshed, out of sight of the camp. Believe it or not, he captured a perfectly acceptable signal from two stations, one in Duluth, Minnesota, 300 miles distant, and the second from Thunder Bay. During the summer when the camp's generator was running he had power for the TV. After the generator was shut down for the season, he used a small gasoline generator which he placed outside his house. When that failed, he rigged up a jerry-built system using an ancient direct-current generator plugged into an alternator he scrounged from the junk pile. Periodically, Joe would remove the back of the TV set and pick around with a screwdriver to fix something or other, amidst frequent showers of sparks and an occasional jolt to himself - this was always done with the set turned on, of course. Why he did not electrocute himself was a great mystery! Joe, in his early years at Owakonze, ran a trapline during the winter with a team of dogs. He had a trapline cabin some twenty miles away and would run the circuit semiweekly. In later years he used a snowmobile and was able to run the entire trapline in a day and be home in time to watch the hockey game! TV, at Owakonze today, has taken on a greater sophistication. Rene has a small satellite dish powered by several solar powered batteries and is able to get better reception than many people who live in cities!

When Joe and Bunnie's children, Rocky and Rene, were of young school age they were home schooled by their mother. The Canadian government had a system set up for educating children in isolated places such as Owakonze. A supervising teacher assisted each student from Toronto, by mail, with most of the work being done by the parents. The lessons were mailed in, the teacher's comments were sent back. The system worked well through about 5th or 6th grade, at which point the boys were sent to live in Atikokan with a family during the school term. They would come back home on the train on holidays and during the summers. It was not an ideal situation, but it worked as well as possible.

Owakonze did not have the only population in the area; there have always been a number of neighbors who live and have lived in the area year around. During the earliest years of Owakonze there were few other inhabitants other than some isolated First Nations people, some of whom lived on a reservation on Lac De Mille Lacs, and served as guides for Camp Windigo when it was in operation. Sometime in the mid 1920's a man named Bob Sawdo arrived. He was quite a character and provided the area with some color and interest. Generations of Owakonze campers were under the mistaken impression that Sawdo was an Indian, but such was not the case. He is believed to have been an American from Michigan's Upper Peninsula, near Bark River. He was, however, married to a full blooded Ojibway Indian woman. They had a number of children, most of whom moved somewhere other than Owakonze as soon as they were able.

Bob Sawdo built a log house below the CNR tracks near the Owakonze station. Then he built several more log buildings on the same site, one of which soon sported a sigh which, impossibly enough, claimed it to be a "hotel"! This was, in fact, a fairly big log building, two stories in height. It never became a hotel; no one ever lived in it, including Sawdo and his wife, and, after fifty or so years, it crumbled away, although signs of it may still be visible today.

Sawdo, though not a big man, was phenomenally strong. The stories of his almost legendary strength were known for hundreds of miles in all directions, and for good reason. One of the Owakonze canoe trips might be as far away from camp as Sioux Lookout and someone would say, "You from Owakonze, eh? You know Bob Sawdo, then? He is one strong feller!" Bob did a bit of fishing, some of it was done illegally, using nets, and hunting, also illegally for the most part, but primarily he was a trapper, usually illegally as well! He was constantly being chased by the Ontario Department of Lands and Forests game wardens from the Quetico Provincial Park, an area protected from poachers. Bob would take furs illegally both inside and outside the park boundaries.

In those days, well before the advent of light aluminum boats, the favorite water craft, other than the canoe, was the "Peterborough" boat, manufactured of cedar strips in eastern Ontario. These handsome boats were ubiquitous until the 1950's. Bob Sawdo had one and, in addition, he always had the biggest outboard motor he could find and always ran it wide open at full throttle. If he knew that the mounties or the provincial police were on his trail, he would carry the boat on his shoulders, the motor in one hand and gas can in the other and, in one trip, take it all over the portage. Normally the Peterborouogh boat would be carried by two people. If there was no portage handy, Sawdo would take this load right through the bush with no trail at all! At one time the mounties had tracked him to a clearing in the middle of the forest, but could find no one there, although there was evidence that Sawdo had been there a short time before. As one policeman leaned against a tree it fell over, and there, beneath the roots, was a large cache of beaver furs. The mounties went around pushing on all the trees in the clearing; tree after tree fell over, concealing more furs beneath!

Sawdo could pick up a full 45-gallon drum of gasoline, about 450 pounds, put it across his knees and carefully lift it down into his boat. Another example of his great strength involved a steel railroad rail, which was stored across some blocks at the station. People would attempt to lift this rail, which weighed 90 pounds per three-foot length, and the rail was 30 feet in length. Sawdo would position himself at the center of this rail, lift it up onto his shoulder, and trot down the station platform with it, turn around and replace it on the blocks. To aid campers on the portage, Bob would pick up two canoes, one on each shoulder; these were 18-foot Peterborough canoes and weighed perhaps 100 pounds each. He would carry both across the portage at the same time.

Sawdo was not a close acquaintance of most of the Owakonze population, with the exception of Don Ickes. He, Sawdo, had a propensity to make off with things not nailed down, gasoline or other items left at the portage for Ditsie. Don was the exception; Sawdo never touched things on Two Mile Island. Bob seldom looked at one straight in the eye; his eyes were bright blue, almost fluorescent, were constantly in motion. His hands were huge and his grip was bone-wrenching. One night, as he was speeding down the lake to the railroad, in the complete darkness, he passed Two Mile Island on the south side, rather than, as customary, on the north side, there was suddenly a great crash. Bob's Peterborough had piled up on a hidden rock, just below the surface of the water. Don grabbed a Coleman lantern and ran down to the water's edge, expecting to find the boat smashed to bits. Bob was sheepishly paddling the boat into the island, and said, when he landed, that, after spending most of his life on Baril Lake, he had never been aware of that particular rock before!

At the far eastern end of Baril Lake, near the portage into Lac Des Mille Lacs, Sawdo had built himself a trapline cabin. In the days before snowmobiles, trappers would frequently build cabins at the far reaches of their assigned traplines in order to have a place to spend the night if they were unable to get back to home base, or if the weather turned bad. Sawdo moved from the west end of the lake to the east at some point and lived from then on in his trapline cabin; it was more convenient for him as his trapline extended into Lac Des Mille Lacs. During his last years he started to take in a few tourists to guide them to fishing spots.

One evening in midsummer, he had a group of fishermen staying with him. He started to go down the lake to the railroad to pick up supplies. He pushed his boat away from the dock and pulled the starting cord on the motor. It started on the first pull; sadly enough Bob always started his motor in gear, standing up. This time the boat suddenly lurched forward and catapulted him over the stern and into deep water, several hundred feet from shore. The unattended motor canted to one side while the boat sped around in circles with Bob in the middle. The horrified fishermen witnessed the entire incident from shore and went out in another boat to rescue him; they had to stop the runaway boat first, which took some time. Bob had gone down by the time they controlled the boat; he could not swim a stroke, which seems odd as he had spent his entire life on the water.

By the time the fishermen realized that Sawdo had drowned it was dark. They had never been on Baril Lake and had no knowledge of Owakonze. After failing to recover the body, they began to paddle a canoe until they came to Two Mile Island, owned by Don Ickes and his family. Don contacted the mounted police with his ham radio. The police directed that the train be met the following morning, since an officer would be aboard. It turned out that the officer was a raw recruit, having just graduated from police training; this was his first real case. He was taken to the site of the accident and they began dragging for the body. The fishermen had had the foresight to mark the spot where they thought the body might be. Three days of dragging proved unsuccessful and, at length, the officer was ordered to return to his base. Ultimately a diver was sent out from Fort William and Bob Sawdo's body was recovered. It was clear that he had been struck by the spinning propeller.

Around 1929 another man arrived at Brule Portage full of mystery and intrigue. Bill Nix is rumored to have been a native of Mississippi and had fled the US to escape the law for something or other. He decided to settle himself at the portage near the station and did so after building a log house for himself and his new wife Lily who was one of Bob Sawdo's daughters. Lily, after enduring many years of dubious marital benefits, living with Bill, who, himself, shared many of Sawdo's extra-legal propensities, departed for parts unknown. Lily returned briefly when Bob's body was recovered from the lake. There was a kind of funeral cortege down the lake with Lily riding in great somber style in the middle of the Peterborough boat, all clad in black mourning garb.

Meanwhile, there was another local family in the immediate area. Frank Tenniscoe, an Ojibway Indian, and his wife produced 19 children, who obviously ranged in age and sex. Frank Tenniscoe was notoriously mean to his family, and whenever he drank too much, his wife would take all the shotgun shells out of their shack and bury them back in the woods to prevent Frank from shooting anyone. Often, an Owakonze canoe trip traveling it's way down Brule Creek would hear the sound of shotgun fire and would know that they would have to hold up until the coast was clear again. As Frank grew older he became more and more ornery and his children tried several times to do him in; they rolled heavy rocks down the railway bridge trestle upon him, they tipped him out of a boat in the middle of Windigoostigwan, the lake down Brule Creek, in an attempt to drown him. All of these attempts were unsuccessful and he died peacefully in the Atikokan Hospital, surrounded by his family.

Bill Nix, by now separated from Lily, had decided that living alone was not such a grand arrangement, so he and Ruth Tenniscoe, one of Frank's many daughters began their relationship which turned into a common-law marriage, and produced four children.

The property owners on Baril Lake in the 1990's are mostly all the second generation Owakonze affiliates, with a couple of exceptions. Robert t. Drake owned a small cabin towards the eastern part of the lake. His grandsons, Wally and Eric Sanford, have taken over his cabin and continue to come up as often as possible. Bill Miller's island, 3 Mile Island, is owned and used by his three daughters, Christine, Mary and

Kimberly, and their families. Bill's wife, Alice still makes the trip north from Wisconsin accompanying one or other of her daughters. Don's island, 2-Mile Island, is owned by his three children, Peter, Alison and Tony, who are up there at least once a year and sometimes even in the winter! George Mangle's property was always owned by his son John Mangle, who continues to go up with his wife, Hilda. His son's also come up occasionally. One notable exception to the Owakonze alumni status is Elmer Baxter and his wife, Deanna, who bought Charlie Montford's cabin near Brule Portage. Charlie, a Canadian from Thunder Bay, had been employed by the camp as a carpenter in the 1960's. When he died Elmer bought his cabin and spends nearly all his free time at the lake, winter and summer. Bill Nix's son, Buddy is also a neighbor. He has build a cabin down by his old family homestead. Buddy leaves Thunder Bay at every opportunity and brings his family out to the lake as well.

Rene Kreis lives full time on the camp island as its caretaker and general handy man. His lifestyle is a great deal more comfortable and updated than it was in his childhood. He is in touch with the outside world by telephone and has his satellite dish to pick up TV. There is another couple, Clyde and Helen Ridell, who live year around on Windigoostigwan. There is much socialization that goes on between all the year round residents; snowmobiles make winter travel quick and easy, except when the snow is too deep! It is a nice feeling that someone is on Baril Lake and being able to enjoy the beauty and solitude when most everyone else is back in a city somewhere.

ICKES' FOLLY AND OTHER PROJECTS

This story begins with a boat used by the camp for many, many years known as "the Gray Boat" for the obvious reason that it was indeed gray. It was powered by an inboard engine in the 1920's. That engine died permanently and was replaced by a new model-A Ford motor converted to marine use by Ted Farrington. Legend has it that the Gray Boat had been originally built in Duluth as a racing boat, and for many years it was the fastest boat on Baril Lake. It was the boat that pulled the aquaplane before water skis became popular. Gray Boat finally reached the end of her career in the late 1960's (?) and, after the engine was removed, was towed into the middle of the lake one night and given a Viking fire funeral to the enjoyment of the campers.

One of Gray Boat's most important jobs was to pull the great barge and the heavy loads it carried, human or otherwise. In latter years it pulled two barges, one alongside the other. Without Gray Boat there was no way to pull the barges, although a number of ideas were tried, but none satisfactory.

One winter, while en-route to Owakonze for one of his frequent winter trips, Don Ickes stopped at the Thunder Bay International Airport to see Orville Weiben, an old friend who ran Superior Airways, a charter flying service sometimes used by the camp. Orville's operation had suffered a bad fire a few weeks previous; his large hangar and shop building had burned to the ground and Don wanted to see the damage before going on to camp. While he was poking around the burned-out building he spotted a large steel boat standing next to the hangar. It had been a Lake Superior fishing boat that had a double steel hull and was powered by a Chrysler marine engine. Out of curiosity Don asked Orville if he'd sell the boat thinking it would be a good replacement for Gray Boat. Orville agreed to sell the boat for $850.

Arrangements were made that Weiben would have responsibility for getting the boat to the freight terminal at the Lakehead (Thunder Bay) and get it loaded on the train. A work crew was at the portage by the station at Owakonze to unload it upon it's arrival. As the "local" rounded the curve in the track and got closer to the station the boat seemed to grow in size on it's flatcar until it looked as big as the Standard Oil building lying on it's side! The winter before the boat had been lying next to a huge hangar building and was covered entirely with snow and had not looked quite so enormous.

The train came to a stop and the entire train crew squatted on their haunches beside the track and watched the process of determining how to unload the behemoth. Of course, the single track line was completely shut down while the "local" was stopped at Owakonze. There were no timbers on the train to use for unloading, so crowbars, pipes for rollers, chain hoists and every other mechanical advantage that could be thought of were used to inch the boat as close to the edge of the flatcar as possible. Fortunately, at the rear end of the train was a "work car", which was used by the railroad for major repairs along the right-of-way. The work car was full of heavy tools, but, most importantly, the man in charge of the work turned out to be related to one of the cooks at camp, and he mustered his men to help the Owakonze work crew. Finally the boat was moved until it was barely teetering on the edge of the flatcar. All of this had taken close to an hour, with the main railroad line still at a dead stop.

There was, by this time, a second truck to supplement Ditsie with all of her portage duties. Both vehicles were backed as close to the track as safety permitted, and chains were run from each to the boat. When the signal was given, drivers in both trucks let out the clutches, spun their wheels and lurched ahead a few inches; it was just enough to make the boat tip off the flatcar and fall like a stone some four feet to the cinders. It was now off the train, but it's gunwales were only an inch or two from the railroad car, which was insufficient clearance to allow the trains to move safely. There was still the problem of pulling the boat another five or so inches away from the track. The work crew was finally successful and the "local" pulled off, doubtless relieved to be rid of Owakonze and all of it's headaches! While technically clear of the tracks, the boat, now resting on the ground, was far too close to leave where it was. Remember the telegrapher who moved even further away than the siding on which his caboose was parked?

Now the real work began. Using rollers, timbers, planks, chains, house jacks, and anything else which might have been of use, the work crew worked to move the boat across the portage. By nightfall the boat had been moved maybe 200 feet away from the railroad tracks. The next day the crew had continued to move it across the quarter mile portage, up hills, down hills, over rocks and stumps and around very sharp curves.

Another full day was spent with the entire work crew on hand and they managed to move the boat a total of 400 feet from the station! It ended the day smack in the middle of the portage road, where Ditsie could not get around it to meet the regular passenger train with milk, mail, food etc. A road had to be cut around the boat to get by it. By this time, most of the mechanical assists were damaged or broken; roller pipes were bent like pretzels, same with the crowbars, transmissions on the two trucks had been hurt, and countless boards and timbers splintered. And there sat the boat.

Joe Kreis, by now the camp caretaker, had spent the three days cursing (in an inimitable manner!) the boat and everything about it. At one point, Joe sat himself down inside a spare tire on the ground and steadfastly stared at the boat, while he chain-smoked one cigarette after another. It was obvious that there was no way the quarter mile portage could be negotiated the way it had been tried. Joe figured out the solution; the next day he brought the camp's complete acetylene welding outfit, including the cutting torch. He was a superlative welder and proceeded at one gunwale to cut down one side of the boat, across the bottom and up the opposite side. When he was finished, one section of the boat fell from the main portion and off into the weeds. Then Joe moved to the other end and repeated the operation; the second part fell off, leaving only the midsection, which was the heaviest since it held the engine. Now each section could slowly be dragged over the portage on timbers and rollers a few feet at a time. When the sections reached Baril Lake they were coaxed onto the barge and hauled into the camp. After three days of this, all three sections made it to camp, even though the last 100 feet before the portage dock was up a very steep hill made of bedrock.

Once at camp, all three sections were careful lined up and Joe re-welded them back together. A new cabin was built to shelter passengers from the rain, and a towing ring was installed on the stern. After tinkering with the engine, the boat went into regular service the next summer and from that year (around 1965) until 1992 did yeoman service on all kinds of camp work details. It could carry more than thirty passengers and a good bit of heavy baggage, while pulling the barge at the same time. The original $850 was probably well spent after all.

Compilation of the History of Owakonze

This saga of Owakonze continues on into the mid 1990's with some major changes on Baril Lake. Most of the old guard have passed away, and with them many of the stories and history. For the children who had the luxury and opportunity to grow up on Baril Lake the memories live on, along with the realization that the next generation will never have the same experiences and stories to listen to over hot cups of coffee in the dining hall. They will have their own experiences and tall tales to share and embellish. It is not certain that any fish they ever catch will ever be as large or plentiful as the one day's catch in the photograph, but it will be as important and exciting as it was decades ago.

There is a poignant sadness that is the final chapter of this monologue. There is a joke in the Ickes family about the passing of the older generation. Don used to bemoan the aging process, and change was never easy for him. When he would, in his own last years, reminisce about Camp he would become pensive and sit in his old lumber camp chair in his log cabin on Two Mile Island, looking down toward the camp island and say, "Duke is dead, Carl is dead, Ted is dead..." later on his family would add to the troubles whenever something would go wrong, so that the phrase became, "Duke is dead, Carl is dead, the donuts didn't rise" etc. To this day that is not an uncommon phrase that is, at once silly, but also instantly conjures up the image of the cabin on the island and Dad and all the memories that is Owakonze.

By rights there should be an entire section included on the amazing people who called Owakonze home for summer after summer. It is too difficult to imagine how to include everyone. A telling moment came in the summer of 1987; it was made very clear what an exceptional place Owakonze really is. 1987 marked the 50th year that Don Ickes spent on Baril Lake (Bill Miller arrived approximately the same year). Don's children, with the help of John and Hilda Mangle, decided to throw a surprise party for him at camp that summer. When the planning was first started, the hope was that maybe 20 or so friends would be able to come and join us for a couple of days. Boy's Hope was gracious enough to let us use "our" camp for the festivities. We began writing letters in January of that year, and were able to get a hold of some of the old camper lists from Gertrude Vollert, the former camp secretary. One letter would lead to another and names and people came crawling out of the woodwork.

By June, it was clear that we were going to have more than 20 people. Figuring out the logistics of getting people into the lake and onto the camp island without Don finding out was a major headache, not to mention all the supplies and hoping for good weather. The surprise of the century occurred when Don went down for a small dinner party on a sunny afternoon in August. 70 people arrived in canoes while Don was on the trip dock! They were heralded with the ringing of the bell in the traditional Owakonze way. In the end, we were able to have people from the 30's, 40's, 50's, 60's, 70,s and 80's all show up. In addition to the 70 that traveled all that way to Ontario, there were cards and letters from all over the US, Canada, and as far away as Italy. The response to the opportunity of being able to revisit Owakonze was truly overwhelming. It spoke volumes about what a treasure it really is.

This narrative has not truly touched the heart of what was and is Owakonze, and that is the many, many people who impacted and left their mark on Baril Lake. For some of the lucky families, the next generation has taken over and is keeping a good watch over things. Granted, much has changed on the different islands and cabins, and not always in the manner in which Don Ickes, Bill Miller, Bob Drake, Joe Kreis, and George Mangle would have done it, but the changes have come with respect and consideration for how they would have liked to have seen things develop. It is likely that every time the present generation does make a change it is with the feeling that their fathers are looking over their shoulder, making sure that it is done to satisfaction.

35

Don is buried on Two Mile Island, Bill Miller is on Three Mile Island, Joe Kreis is somewhere at Owakonze and George Mangle is down at his cabin. We take solace and satisfaction that these four men are still up there watching over the place, and probably still arguing over whose piece of driftwood it really is that is hanging in the cabin! There is a story that Don's ghost was spotted the summer he passed away. A young man who worked for Boy's Hope was a passionate piano player. He spent time tuning and fixing up Don's old piano. One evening, after the generator was turned off, he was playing honky tonk piano (Don's favorite kind of playing), when a figure appeared at the end of the dining hall. The figure moved closer to the piano, at which time the player got scared and took off. He told Rene Kreis about it, who assured him that it was only Don checking on things. There is also an eagle who appeared at the end of the lake the day Don's ashes arrived. The timing of the bird's flight seemed to indicate that Don was there. The eagle has made it's presence known every time any of the family is on the island. It flies over as if it is checking everything over and giving the family a stamp of approval.

Who knows what really is happening, but many of us have taken comfort that the history does live on and continues to grow.

Merry
Christmas

ETHEL AND CARL ANDERSON

Season's
Greetings

Camp
OWAKONZE
Limited

HARVEY F. DICKINSON, CAMP DIRECTOR
121 WEST NINTH STREET
HINSDALE, ILLINOIS—TEL. FAculty 3-3063

WINNETKA OFFICE—P. O. BOX 129
WINNETKA, ILLINOIS
TEL. HILLcrest 6-0639

OWAKONZE, ONTARIO, CANADA

Location

The Camp is on an island in Baril Lake in western Ontario, approximately 70 miles north of the international boundary. It has its own post office and railway station on the Canadian National Railway between Port Arthur and Fort Frances. There is rail transportation directly to the Camp plus bus, automobile, and airline transportation to points nearby.

Climate

An invigorating climate. Days are about like northern Wisconsin. Nights are cool, sometimes cold — wonderful for sleeping. Water temperature is around 70 degrees. There is no hay fever. Owakonze is an ideal place for sufferers from hay fever and asthma.

HUBACHEK & KELLY
919 NORTH MICHIGAN AVENUE
CHICAGO
ZONE 11

September 30, 1955

Mr. Roger F. A. Thew
Safety and Training Director
Steep Rock Iron Mines Limited
Steep Rock Lake, Ontario

Dear Roger:

I have procured copies of the pictures of the Dawson relics referred to in my letter of September 27th. I am send-   *
ing them to you herewith.

These pictures will require some explanation, however, and I will try to give you an account of my understanding concerning each. You will note that I have written a number on the back of each picture.

No. 1 is a wagon wheel and horse shoe which was removed from the lake this summer at the point which we have discussed in previous correspondence. The wagon wheel is of a very old type construction according to one of the camp carpenters and the horse shoe is too small to have been fitted to any horses used in the past by the Camp. Note the barnacles on the metal rim of the wheel.

I might inject here a comment concerning these old metal objects. I am told by some people who have had some experience along this line that when some of these old objects are removed from the water they appear to be quite well preserved considering the length of time they have been submerged. But once exposed to the air I understand that they disintegrate rapidly and frequently they turn to powder in a relatively short period of time. I understand that this wagon wheel mentioned above is already deteriorating, thus it might be in order to investigate the methods which the archeologists use to preserve items for historical purposes if it is hoped to place them in some museum.

No. 2 shows five small items. The largest of these is a horse shoe which is so encrusted with barnacles that it is firmly affixed to a rock which was also removed from the lake. I believe this came from the island location on Baril

Lake. I believe the other barnacle encrusted object is
a snuff box, but I am not sure. The spike appears to be
a railroad type of spike possibly used on one of Dawson's
narrow gauge railroads. I do not know where the nut and
bolt came from. Possibly Carl Anderson can tell you.

Nos. 3 and 4 are shots of old narrow gauge railroad wheels.
These were found in Baril Lake very close to the dock
of the Baril to Brule Lake Portage which crosses the railroad. I am told that they were seen during a very low
water summer and pulled out from a location approximately
100 feet northwest of this dock. The shaft protruding
from the wheels with the holes in it is not authentic.
These wheels were used to hold volley ball net posts
in connection with Camp activities and undoubtedly that
is the purpose of the shaft for that particular wheel.

No. 5 is a shot of an old chest which was brought in by an
Owakonze canoe trip. I believe it came from the Lac de
Mille Lacs area, possibly the area of the portage from
Baril to Lac de Mille Lacs. I have no idea how to date
this particular object.

Nos. 6 and 7 show an old wooden structure held together by strap
iron and some kind of rods or bolts. Also shown are a
couple of square metal frames plus a couple of very old
type axes.. The wooden structure and the square metal
frames were removed from a Dawson barge which is evidently
sunk near the Baril to Lac de Mille Lacs portage on the
Baril end. The wooden structure was evidently the rudder
of the barge and the metal frames evidently held the shaft
around which the rudder moved. I believe there is still
some evidence of this barge at that location but I do not
know. The two ax heads in these pictures are of the very
old type. Even I can see that. I am told that these two
ax heads were brought in on the same trip that brought in
the wood and metal chest shown in picture 5.

Thus I do not want you to get the impression that all
these objects come from the location next to the Camp's island
in Baril Lake. They all seem to have some historical significance, however, and I thought you would like to see them. I
believe all of these objects are located on the Camp's island
and Carl Anderson can certainly show them to you. Possibly he
can show you a number of other such items, too.

In considering things such as this I suppose one should
bear in mind the fact that a railroad was built in the area and
the area was also logged in the interval between Dawson's day

and the present time. I understand that Baril Lake was logged around the turn of the century and that the big hoist from Baril to Lac de Mille Lacs which is still quite evident was built about that time. Undoubtedly there are many relics to be found from the logging days and days when the railroad was being constructed. A person schooled in these things, however, can differentiate between Dawson's relics and the relics from the later events.

I am going to send a copy of this letter to a number of people, including one Erwin C. Gerber. Mr. Gerber was a staff man at Owakonze for several years and he still goes up there to visit the Camp on occasion. His experiences in the area aroused his interest in the historical significance of such things as these relics we are talking about now. It is quite possible that Mr. Gerber would have some comments to make concerning this letter and some suggestions as to where other such items could be found. Thus you might hear from Mr. Gerber in the future. As a matter of fact, you might have met him in recent years in connection with a visit by the Camp Owakonze groups to the Atikokan area.

Another point I forgot to mention above was a comment I heard concerning the location near the Island on Baril Lake. In 1937 or 1938 Camp Owakonze had a very serious fire which destroyed its administration building and dining hall. In the process of cleaning up after this fire a great deal of debris was sunk into the lake and some of this was evidently dumped in off the small island. Thus there might be some more recent items mixed up with the Dawson items that would be attributable to the Owakonze fire.

After you have looked over the enclosed pictures I would very much appreciate your sending them to Don O'Hearn who could file them with the records and possessions of the Quetico-Superior Foundation. I am sending Don a copy of this letter and I am also enclosing an extra copy for you in case you would like to pass it along to Mr. Fotheringham. I certainly hope that these efforts are productive and I feel certain that this will be a valuable contribution to the work that is being done to realize more of the historical and recreational values of the Quetico-Superior area.

Very truly yours,

F. B. Hubachek, Jr.

es

cc: Messrs. Don O'Hearn
    Carl Anderson
    Erwin C. Gerber

1290 Van Buren Avenue
Saint Paul 4, Minnesota
November 3, 1955

Mr. Frank B. Hubachek, Jr.,
Hubachek and Kelly
919 North Michigan Avenue
Chicago 11, Illinois

Dear Bill:--

It was pleasant to hear from you and to know that you, too,
are interested in the history of the old Dawson Road. I was glad that
my October 7th letter gave you some needed data. I only wish that I
could show you all the material I have dug up, some of which, of course,
I shall use in the book, but much of which will have to be summarized.
For instance, I have the reports sent back year by year by Dawson and
others. I also have quite a number of actual pictures, not photographs
but drawings made by press artists who accompanied expeditions over the
Road. If I get down to Chicago this winter, I will bring some of this
material with me. There are pictures of some of the carts, the barges,
the tugs, the corduroy roads, the houses put up on the portages, and so
forth. I rather expect to get to Toronto this winter to go through a
set of diaries kept by a member of one of the expeditions. I believe
the very first contingent of Mounties went over the Road in the early
1870s. The most famous of all the expeditions, however, was Garnet Wol-
esley's (with 1400 soldiers) in 1870, the so-called Red River expedition
of 1870.

Thank you for keeping me up to date with the correspondence over
the relics. I shall be greatly interested in the results of the diving
activities. I should think it would have been cold for frogmen up there
in late October. Brrrrrr! I am returning the correspondence herewith.
Some of it I had already seen. Mr. Gerber has sent me a lot of data, too.
I am also writing to him this morning.

I had almost forgotten the first draft of an article on the Dawson
Road that I sent to your father two or three years ago. Since then I have
turned up so much new data, that the account is only a skeleton of what
I shall attempt later in the book.

You ask for comments and one thing comes to mind immediately. Of
course the carts could have had metal rims in the 1870s, most likely iron
but quite possibly steel. Steel didn't become common or inexpensive until
the 1880s, but the United States had big iron works by that time. The
Michigan mines were opened in the 1850s and were supplying the Eastern
furnaces with all they could use at that time, aside from the steel, mostly
imported from Great Britain until the open hearth process was perfected
and allowed our Minnesota iron ores to be utilized. You will recall that
our Vermilion range began to ship ore in 1884, because the new process
could make use of our particular kind of ore by that time. I always remember the date for the first general shipping of ore from Lake Superior by
the date of the opening of the Sault Ste Marie lock -- 1855, just a hundred
years ago. The lock was built mostly to enable iron ore to be shipped.

Cordially,

N/n

Grace Lee Nute

P.S. The new edition of The Voyageur
is just coming off the press!
gln

Artifacts from the Dawson Trail.
Photographs taken by F.B. Hubachek

Artifacts from the Dawson Trail.
Photographs taken by F.B. Hubachek

Artifacts from the Dawson Trail.
Photographs taken by F.B. Hubachek

Log Cabin in the foreground is believed
to predate Owakonze structures. At
the time of this photograph (1920s),
it was used as the camp ice-house.

Brule Portage, 1919 or 1920, hauling load by hand near top of hill at Baril Lake.

The first portage dock. 1919 or 1920. Duke is standing in the boat holding a paddle.

1919 or 1920, these are some early scenes at Brule Portage before it was called Owakonze.

Note the man-power before the horse or Ditsie. These were taken before a building was at Milepost 101.

Early lake crossing on barge, 1920's. Note the horse power on barge.

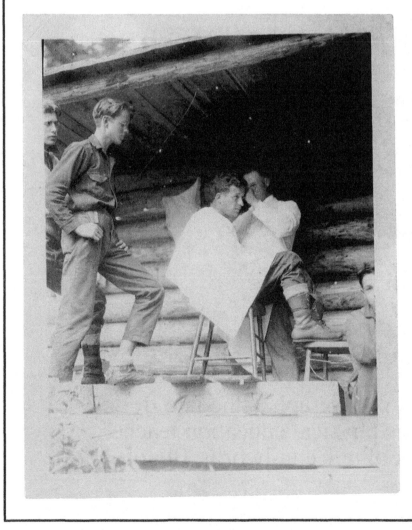

1920's, Duke took this picture of Rae Stout, the camp caretaker being the camp barber.

Early 1920's, clearing for the ball field.

The staff man in this photograph is the late Bob
Townley who was the physical education teacher
at Joseph Sears School in Kennilworth, Illinois.

These photographs were taken in the early 1920's and show the clearing work for the ball field. the horse is probably Dan.

1920 or 1921, building the ballfield pick by
pick and wheel barrow by wheel barrow.

1920 or 1921 building
the ball field with the
1917 Cletrac Tractor.

Lumber cut for
building buildings.
This is back
where the Junior
Camp was located.

Bob Townley is in
the left background.
The horse is Dan.

1922-1923, Church Service on small
island. Duke is in white shirt against the
rocks on the left. His partner, Kewpie
Cragun is at organ.

Duke with a group of campers. Date (?)

Above: 1920's basketball court activities. Bob Townley is on the left.

Left: Badminton. Date ?

This photograph shows the method that was used to bring the ice. The vertical pole supported a long horizontal pole, which in turns carried the ice tongs. The pole was raised, the tongs grabbed a piece of ice, and the operator's weight on the opposite end of the pole raised the ice to the ramp in the background. Then the blocks, each weighing more than 200 pounds, were slid into the ice house and packed with dry sawdust. Visible on the ice at the right are the ice saw, a "spud", or ice-chisel, and a broom. Before cutting, the ice must be swept free of snow for a period of time so it would freeze thick. the man in the photo is Rae Stout.

C boats sailing in
the 1920's.

Canoe Regattas, 1920s (?).

Racing Shell built by the Pocock Company,
Seattle, Washington.

Horse Shoe Pit on Small Island

Duke (far right) giving pep talk before a canoe trip. 1920s.

Bill Riche in middle, Rae Stout on right.

1920s, Duke's toothbrushes.

Looking across from the unfinished canoe dock to the unfinished dining hall. Note the method of constructing the log retaining wall, later filled in with gravel.

This is a picture of the old dining hall and administration building. It burned completely in a fire which occurred during the winter of 1940. The dining hall was to the right, the Camp office to the left. Around the corner, out of the picture was the trip room. The old trip dock projected out into the harbor in the direction of the boat house, right where the big rock is located. A porch ran entirely around the two sides of this building. In the background is the old boathouse which was rebuilt on the same site in 1958. The man standing on the bridge is probably Rae Stout, caretaker for many years.

These photographs were taken several years apart aned show the Clubhouse in different stages of construction.

The stage was build first on the site of a preexisting building. The gym and main floor were added in 1936 and 1937. The woman is Eunice Martin.

The Club House

Rae Stout
Early Caretaker

Ervin C. Gerber
"Gerg", naturalist,
swimming instructor,
canoe trip leader,
astronomer and
Jack-of-all-Learning.

Old Swim Dock off Small Island, 1930's

BILL HALL PETE JOHN MIKE SANDY
SNYDER CLARK FRANTZEN BOZELL PANTHER SANDVIG
ED STAN
OLVER SWANN
SON
OTTO AGATE FRED JOE DUKE
JORDI MARTIN HENSCHEL SCHMITT CHILDS
D.C.

A single day's catch in 1938. Agate Martin and Joe Schimtt.

Banquet on Small
Island - 1930s

Trampoline
1937

Minstral Show
1930s

Winter 1945

Basketball Court, built in the 1940's,

Original
Dininghall
and bridge

Bridge and
burned out
dininghall
1946

THE CLUBHOUSE · OWAKONZE

Kitchen and
Post Office
(right)

"Boar's Nest",
built 1945
(left)

Rifle range on mainland,
north of camp island,
accessable by bridge.
Gerb is the man in the
photo. Rifle range
was later moved behind
the middler camp.

Right, clay tennis courts
by dininghall.

The "Dutchess", 1938.
Below: Carl driving
Grey Boat, towing Liza
and other boat full of
lumber. Date ?

CAMP OWAKONZE LTD.,
CARL & ETHEL ANDERSON CANADA.
(CARETAKERS)

Liza, above,
towing the
barge full of
campers.
Below: Grey
Boat towing
the same barge.
Dates ?

1940, Don Ickes on water slide.

Ethel Anderson
Winter 1940s

Top: Carl and Ethel Anderson summer 1947.
Bottom: In front of their house (built in 1936),
Summer, 1950s

Carl and "Ditsie", and Little Pete Frantzen
Dates (?)

Carl and Ethel Anderson. Below left was taken in 1946. Below right is Ethel (on left) her mother, "Ma" Tillberg, and her sister, Esther Mignault.

CARL & ETHEL ANDERSON

Winter at Owakonze. Above: Anderson Hall.
Below: Dining Hall, Kitchen and Office

Don Ickes

Eleanor Ickes

Ted Farrington
photographs
1952

Winter Scenes. Ethel on
Joe's dog sled.

AXEL & PHYLLIS YOUNGQUIST

Axel and Phyllis Youngquist, late 1950's ?

ETHEL ANDERSON, — PHYLLIS FOSTER — ADELE SUNDBERG —

Camp Cooks at the Banquet
1950s

1958, building new
boat house on same site
as old one.

The new boat house
was larger than the
old, but used some
of the same cribs
and underpinnings.

The new boat house
was completed in four
to five weeks, including
demolishing old one.
Picture shows campers
with barge load of rocks
for cribs.

Ethel Anderson at portage cabin. 1959

Carl Anderson demonstrating use of the broadaxe 1960 (?)

DON ICKES

DON ICKES

Upper left: Campsite on North Arm
July 1961

Left:
Speed boat
donated by
Bill Ross,
(1962 (?)

ESWRAY - TED FARRINGTON, BUILDER & DRIVER

Water sports. Aqua-planning behind speed boat off the trip dock. Playing in the water behind Carl Anderson driv-in the Grey Boat. Dates 1950's & 1960's?

Pete and Little Pete Frantzen
Early 1960s (?)

BOB HANSON   DON ICKES

New Light Plant (Power House)
Bob "Curly" Hanson and Don Ickes
1963

MAKING "BUZZ BRUNING AWARDS"

Norm Chimenti   Ben Kurand   Steve Kling

Making Buzz Bruning Awards for the end of the
summer Baquet, 1963.

F. Neir

A cabin group in the early 1960's. Fran Neir is the staffman at right rear. Peter Ickes is camper at lower right.

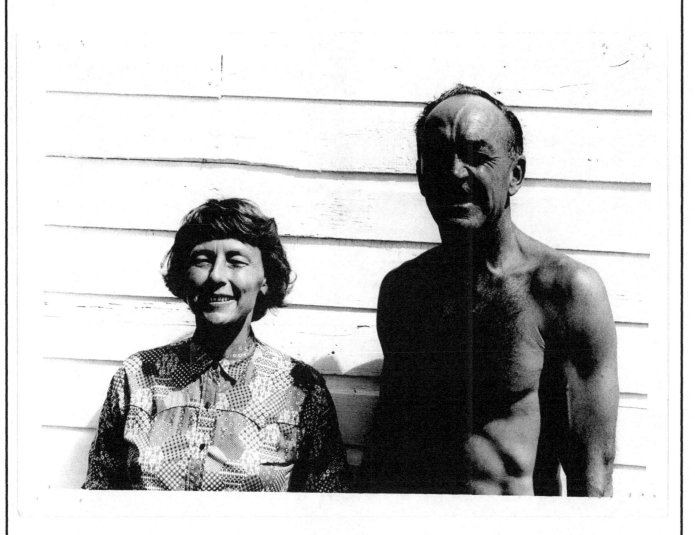

Harvey and Arlene Dickinson
1963

Most of Camp Owakonze Ltd, Stockholders, 1964

Joe and Bunnie Kreis
cutting ice.

The Camp Club House. This is used for indoor athletics including basketball and badminton, Camp shows, and a variety of other activities.

The pleasure of real water thrills — with safety. Our fabulous water toboggan.

Our main swimming dock.

This is included to show the waterslide.

Fall and winter in the 1960's. Above: Jimmy Portalance, Rene and Joe Kreis. Joe with a large fish, and with Tony in March 1968.

The "Icky", 1917 Cletrac Tractor and other machinery, taken in the late 1960's.

"Satisfaction Works, Ltd." work crew 1969, JimKurtz, Jim and Jerry Clifford and Don on the "Icky". Herb Eckhouse, Trey (Frank) Hussey and Mike Kozak in front row.

MAKING TRIP TO JAMES BAY BY CANOE

950-Mile Water Trip
Is Begun by US Youths

By JACK SNIDER

If there's grass-root canoe country anywhere on earth Northwestern Ontario provides it in a manner second to none. Too few of us living in this splendorous panorama of river and lake amid fascinating forests perfumed with historical fragrance are aware of our unparalleled heritage.

It's usually the other fellow who appreciates most what we have and take for granted.

Something is under way at the moment akin to that situation. Friday, four canoes with eight Americn youths in charge of two adults left Sioux Lookout on a journey northward of some 950 miles that will see them paddling salt water as well as fresh along the way.

Their schedule is rigid and itinerary tight. They plan to make the trip in 40 days and end at Moosonee. Scheduled arrival there is Aug. 10-11. Before they're f i n i s h e d they'll have paddled some 100 miles on salt water along the southwest coastline of James Bay from Fort Albany to Moosonee.

WELL TRAINED

All these lads are expert canoeists and experienced wilderness travellers. They learned the hard way under strict supervision, rigid discipline and smack in the harness.

Every summer for several years past they've spent their school vacations being trained for just such an exploit and on-the-scene training has been accomplished here.

The boys are patrons of Camp Owakonze established on Baril lake south of Lac des Mille Lacs 45 years ago as a small group of tents. It now represents a $125,000 investment owned and operated by a corporate body of parents who took this same wilderness training as boys years ago.

In charge of the current big jaunt are F. B. Hubachek Jr., and Don Williamson.

Business obligations in Chicago area prevent lawyer Hubachek from completing the trip and on July 17 Superior Airways will fly Steve Kling to relieve him at Miministka lake in the Albany river country.

Briefly the route from Sioux Lookout is to Osnaburgh House on Lake St. Joseph where rises the historic Albany river and thence along that great waterway to Fort Hope, Ogoki and Fort Albany at river's mouth. Next it's along the coastal waters of James Bay to Moosonee where the paddling will end.

There they will take the Ontario Northland Railway to Cochrane and then by truck to Fort William to board a CNR train here for Owakonze.

Yong paddlers providing their own motive power are Mark Anderson, Rochester, Minn.; Peter Ickes, Winnetka, Ill.; Bill Dickinson, Hindale, Ill.; Bill Habachek, Glencoe, Ill.; Rob Stickler, Des Moines, Iowa; John Sanders, Wilmette, Ill.; John Hanson, Escanaba, Mich., and Skip Welles, Mt. Cisco, NY.

They will keep a meticulous day-by-day journal while en route and we bet it'll be a dandy. It should prove another document of Northwestern Ontario wilderness areas worthy of preservation.

Returning canoe trips. Bottom: Charlie Smith and Peter Ickes returning from Advanced Trip 1967.

A Welcome Sight!

Joe Kreis, 1970.

Above: Launching "Ickes Folly"

"Ickes Folly", welded back together before the cabin was built.

SEPT 3 1972

1973

Barney Swett (l), Camp Director in the 1970s,
just returned from a canoe trip

Father Paul Sheridan and Joe Kreis
Boy's Hope Owakonze

Joe and Dink Kreis
1980s

Joe and Dink Kreis

Middler Staff 1961

Fran Neir's Middler Cabin

Advanced Trip 1967

Advanced Trip 1968

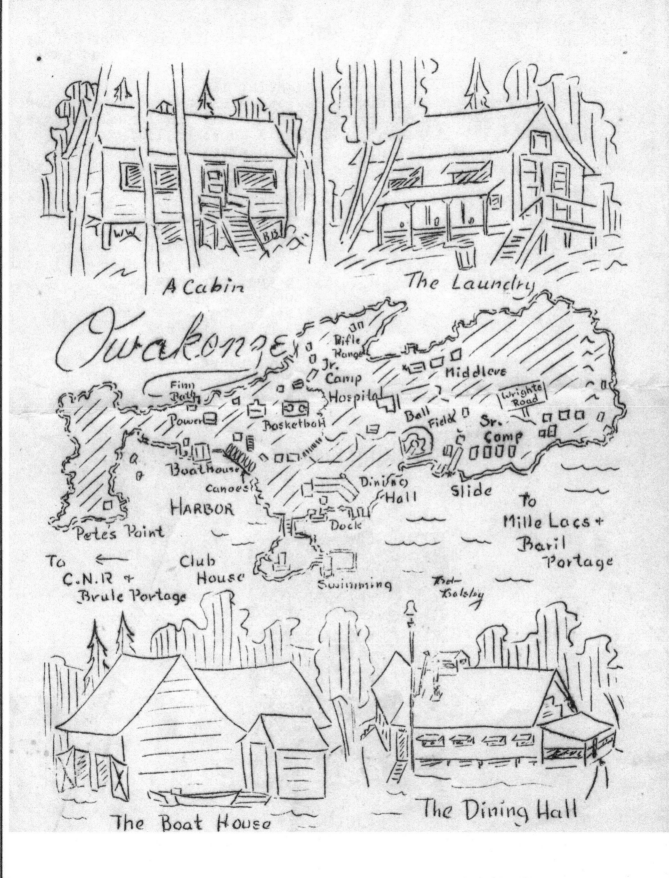

A Cabin

The Laundry

Owakonze

Rifle Range

Jr. Camp

Hospital

Middlero

Finn Bath

Wright Road

Power

Basketball

Ball Field

Sr. Camp

Boathouse

Canoes

Dining Hall

Slide

HARBOR

Pete's Point

Dock

To
Mille Lacs +
Baril
Portage

To
C.N.R +
Brule Portage

Club House

Swimming

Bel-
Balsley

The Boat House

The Dining Hall

To Wear		To Carry In Pack Or Duffel
Boots or Work Shoes (Greased)		RAIN GEAR
Wool sox		Pack sack with tump - or duffel
Undershorts		and tump
Undershirts		Rubberized liner bag
Blue jeans		Sleeping bag
Long sleeve shirt	(Bandana)	Sweat shirt and sweat pants (or
Belt	(Compass)	flannel pajamas)
Handkerchief	(Match case)	Tennis shoes or loafers
Hat	(Knife)	3 or 4 extra pairs wool sox
"Pocket Ammunition"	(Map)	1 extra undershorts and undershirt
		1 extra blue jeans

Other Items

Paddle
(Life vest)
(Rod - lash in the canoe)

1 extra shirt
4 extra handkerchiefs
Jacket or sweater
Toilet kit in ditty bag - soap,
   tooth brush, tooth powder, comb,
   chapstick, nose plug
Towel   (Camera)
Flashlight   (Cord)
(Reel and fish tackle)
(Air mattress)
(Boot grease)

Packing List

"Gerb"

The education of receiving the Big Pot

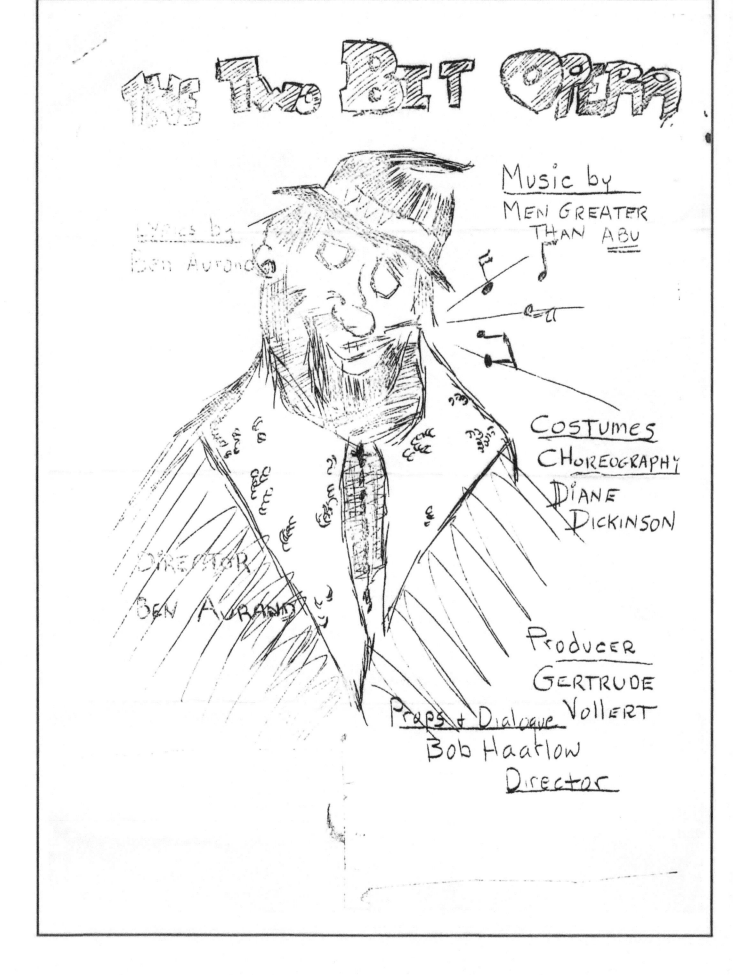

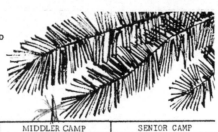

CAMP OWAKONZE LIMITED
Camp Calendar
1962

DAY		JUNIOR CAMP	MIDDLER CAMP	SENIOR CAMP
June 27	Weds	←	Campers Leave Chicago	→
28	Thurs	←	Campers Arrive Owakonze	→
29	Fri	←	Orientation	→
30	Sat	←	Orientation	→
July 1	Sun	←	All Boys in Camp	→
2	Mon	3-Day Canoe Trip	Middlers in Camp	4-Day Canoe Trip
3	Tues			
4	Weds			
5	Thurs	Juniors in Camp	4-Day Canoe Trip	
6	Fri			Seniors in Camp
7	Sat			
8	Sun			
9	Mon		Middlers in Camp	
10	Tues			
11	Weds	5-Day Canoe Trip		
12	Thurs			
13	Fri			
14	Sat			8-Day Canoe Trip
15	Sun			
16	Mon	Juniors in Camp	6-Day Canoe Trip	
17	Tues			
18	Weds			
19	Thurs			
20	Fri			
21	Sat			
22	Sun	2d Sess. Lv. Chgo. ←→	Middlers in Camp ←→	2d Sess. Lv. Chgo.
23	Mon	2d Session Arrive Owakonze ←→		
24	Tues	←	1st Session Leave Owakonze	→
25	Weds	←	Orientation and Program	→
26	Thurs	4-Day Canoe Trip	4-Day Canoe Trip	4-Day Canoe Trip
27	Fri		(Optional for Full Season Campers)	
28	Sat			
29	Sun			
30	Mon	All Juniors in Camp	All Middlers in Camp	All Seniors in Camp
31	Tues			
Aug 1	Weds			
2	Thurs			10-12 Day Canoe Trip
3	Fri			
4	Sat		8 or 10 Day Canoe Trip	
5	Sun			
6	Mon	6 or 8 Day Canoe Trip		
7	Tues			
8	Weds			
9	Thurs			
10	Fri			
11	Sat			
12	Sun			
13	Mon			
14	Tues	←	Final Camp Fire - Individual Sports	→
15	Weds	←	Final Camp Show - Individual Sports	→
16	Thurs	←	Camp Banquet - Individual Sports	→
17	Fri	←	All Campers Depart	→
18	Sat	←	Campers Arrive Chicago	→

Harvey F. Dickinson, Director
121 W. Ninth St., Hinsdale, Ill.
Phone: FA 3-3063
Gertrude Vollert
2608 Greenleaf, Wilmette, Ill.
Phone: AL 1-5145

Notes

Camp Owakonze, Ltd.
Owakonze, Ontario, Canada
Phone: Owakonze 924

A very early Owakonze brochure

The O-wa-kon-ze Camps

Everything boys like to do under ideal conditions and competent supervision in the

Finest Camping Country in America

W. L. CHILDS, Director

Head of Department of Physical Education, New Trier High School, Winnetka, Illinois

Member National Camp Directors' Association
Charter Member Mid-West Camp Directors' Association

SUMMER ADDRESS:
O-wa-kon-ze, Ontario

WINTER ADDRESS:
1578 Oak Ave., Evanston, Ill.

UNDER PRESENT MANAGEMENT SINCE 1919

O-wa-kon-ze
for Boys

❦

Purpose

First View of Camp

Not Just an Outing—Not a School—but a Wonderful Opportunity for the Development of All Manly Qualities

"How shall my boy spend the summer?" This is a problem of greatest concern to every parent who has the best interest of the boy at heart—a problem which for many years O-wa-kon-ze has been helping to solve to the satisfaction of parents and boys alike. Surely there can be but one answer. The boy must have a complete change and a change to the kind of life which will best meet the needs of a normal, fast growing boy.

The boy's greatest need at this time is for ideal conditions for growth, for health and for the development of social adjustments. He needs outdoor life, he needs to break away from the environment where everything is done for him. He needs to be put on his own, to develop his own individuality through playing a real part in a life which he can understand.

He needs the companionship of boys of his own age, the discipline of sports, a training in fair play, the discipline which comes through the intimate association with clear eyed, clean minded boys, the friendly counsel of men of character and experience, the watchful care of experts in boy training who are always on the job.

He needs the development of many interests through a program of widely varied activities which have a strong appeal to boys, a vigorous life on which to spend his surplus energy and a complete change from the life of the winter months.

He needs the development of right habits of living, he needs to learn the joy of achievement, the satisfaction that comes from the knowledge of work well done; he needs to develop the faculty of making friends and the habit of making good in whatever things he undertakes. He needs to establish a work habit, and this under conditions where work is a joy, where the good of the boy and the boy's happiness are always the first consideration.

These things are not to be found in the city, at a summer resort, touring the country, on a farm or at a private home. They are found only in properly conducted, highly organized, private camps.

To provide ideal conditions along the lines suggested above has been the constant aim of the director of the O-wa-kon-ze Camps.

"The properly conducted organized camp is the most important step in education America has given the world."—Dr. Chas. W. Eliot, Former President Harvard University.

*Life at Camp O-wa-kon-ze
Develops Vigorous
Constitutions and Sterling
Character*

Never-to-be-forgotten Nights Around the Campfire

Real Cruising. They Come Back Hard as Nails

The purpose which Camp O-wa-kon-ze serves, and for which it was organized, is to supply certain needs in the life of boys which are not ordinarily met by present day living conditions and the usual methods of education.

Our country occupies a high place among the nations of the world because of the hardy pioneers who made it what it is. Men like Abraham Lincoln and Cyrus McCormick, a race of men who lived in the open, and daily went through long hours of hard work with their hands and with their muscles, developed iron constitutions and iron nerves and passed on to succeeding generations a fund of splendid vitality. It is for us to see that this fund is kept intact— a permanent endowment for future generations.

The great development of machinery has robbed us of the natural physical exercise which gave our forefathers their splendid constitutions. The comfort of our homes and offices keeps us indoors, away from the invigorating influence of fresh air and sunshine. The automobile removes the necessity of walking. The complex and intense life of the city is a great drain upon the nervous system. While modern science has greatly reduced the amount of sickness from contagious diseases in recent years, the increase in nervous disorders and functional diseases is appalling. Jacob Riis says, "Civilization is making of the world a hothouse." There is danger that our boys grow up like hothouse plants. They need outdoor living to make them hardy and vigorous.

We have a problem of keeping physically fit which was unknown to our grandfathers, a problem which must be met by exercise, life in the open and more wholesome conditions of living. Camp O-wa-kon-ze aims to supply this need in present day civilization, and to add a training in character building, a difficult and immensely important problem of education. Camp life is peculiarly adapted to the development of certain traits of character which our ancestors possessed in a high degree and which we covet for the young men of to-day.

Such qualities as courage, honesty, unselfishness, co-operation, ambition, control of temper, determination, (O-wa-kon-ze is the Dakotah Indian word for determination) perseverance, resourcefulness, initiative and self-reliance are important elements of character which can be developed, and which are, perhaps, better developed through athletic sports and through a training in meeting the conditions of primitive life than in any other way.

"The ideal life for a boy is not in the city. He should know of animals, rivers, plants, and that great out-of-door life that lays for him the foundation of his later years." Dr. G. Stanley Hall.

Cruising Through the Quetico

Camping in the Quetico Country

A big experience for a boy. A man-making summer of real sport and real camping in an ideal camping country, untouched by civilization, far removed from towns and summer resorts, at one of the best equipped camps in America, under the leadership of men of unquestioned character and refinement, men of ability and experience in teaching and dealing with boys, experts, enthusiasts and real leaders in the various activities promoted at the camp. A health, strength and character building summer, full of joyful activity and exciting experiences. A wonderful chapter in the life of any boy. This Camp O-wa-kon-ze offers.

Location

The camp is situated on Baril Lake, a beautiful lake in the center of a wonderful camping country. It lies almost due north of Duluth, Minnesota, is 766 miles from Chicago and about 70 miles north of the international boundary. Baril Lake is the natural gateway to the Quetico Forest Preserve and is the connecting link between the Quetico Reserve on the west and the wonderful Mille Lacs country on the east. For a hundred miles in every direction from the camp stretches a country of pine forests, lakes and streams yet untouched by civilization save where the railroad connecting Port Arthur and Winnipeg cuts directly through it. All travel is by canoe and portage, the methods used by the Indians for centuries.

The country is one of great natural beauty and full of historic interest. Our trips go over the routes made by the Indians ages before the coming of the white man. "The chains of lakes, linked together by rivers and streams, are from the canoeist's standpoint the most famous on the continent."

Throughout this district and farther go our boy explorers. Through the Quetico and Superior National Forests on the south, from Lake Shabandowan on the east, from Lac Seul and the English River on the north, to the Lake of the Woods on the west the O-wa-kon-ze blazes point the way for those who follow after.

"Nature is a school for the hardier virtues."—Grover Cleveland.

The Camp Site

The choice of the camp site was a particularly happy one. It is in the center of the finest canoeing country in America, the starting point for many entrancing canoe trips in all directions. It is in a district so wild that it is little frequented by tourists or others, yet thanks to the through train service it is within easy reach of civilization.

The camp occupies two islands comprising thirty-two acres of beautiful woodland near the north shore of Baril Lake. This is an attractive lake, ten miles long, with deeply indented bays and high shores covered with spruce, balsam, pine and some birch and poplar. The lake is sufficiently narrow and broken by islands to be a safe lake at all times.

The invigorating climate, the just right summer temperature, the high altitude and the health giving properties of an atmosphere saturated with pine and balsam, all contribute toward an ideal location.

The camp occupies the highest point in the vicinity. The altitude is 1,700 feet. From Baril Lake the water sheds in three directions, north to Hudson's Bay, southeast to Lake Superior and west to the Lake of the Woods.

Owing to the high altitude, the high shore lines, the rocky character of the soil and the island location of the camp, far removed from swampy districts, we are troubled very little by mosquitoes. The lake water is clear and the swimming excellent. Temperature tests taken during the summer of 1921 showed Baril Lake to maintain a temperature of 72 degrees Fahrenheit during the camping season.

"The summer camp is the most important institution available for personality training."—Dr. English Bagby, Uni. of North Carolina.

In the Heart of America's Finest Camping Country

Camp Equipment

Believing that the boys have enough of the "roughing it" of pioneer life on the trips, the equipment of the permanent camp home has been designed to furnish comfort and convenience, and to give the greatest possible opportunity for pleasure and good times. The physical equipment represents a valuation of over $60,000.00.

Administration Buildings

Buildings

The equipment includes forty-two buildings. There is a large log club house with a huge fireplace and a large frame game building for evenings and rainy days. There is a photographic studio, a large boat house and an ice house with an ample supply of ice. All boys are housed in roomy well built frame cabins and supplied with first class Simmons steel spring beds and mattresses.

Boats

The camp has a fine fleet of boats, including two large motor boats, seven outboard motorboats, rowboats, four sailboats, fifty canoes, two large barges and a four-oared racing shell.

Athletic Equipment

There is an excellent athletic field equipped for baseball, playground ball, soccer and tennis. The game equipment includes a concrete handball court, four paddle tennis courts, a gymnasium floor 60 by 100 feet in size, equipped for basketball and volley ball,

boxing and wrestling rings, etc. There is a tramplin table, a tight rope, a 120 foot water toboggan slide and an enclosed swimming pool equipped with two diving towers and three good springboards. There is a rifle range with steel boiler plate backstop and a shelter for the shooters.

Water Supply

Excellent drinking water is supplied by the camp well. A pumping plant and elevated water tank supply running water to the camp.

Milk

Milk is obtained from the Port Arthur Dairy and is pasteurized.

Electric Lights

The camp has its own electric lighting system which supplies light to buildings, bridge and paths.

Sanitation

The sanitation is in charge of the camp physician. It has been inspected by and has met the approval of the Provincial Inspector of Camps. Kaustine Chemical Toilets are used throughout the camp.

Trip Equipment

The trip equipment is the best obtainable. The tents used are Baker style, made of light khaki colored waterproof material, with sewed in mosquito fronts, and floored with heavy waterproof groundcloth. The cooking outfits and other trip requisites are the latest thing in camp equipment.

Organization

Although together for meals, sports and social affairs, there are five distinct divisions of the camp family. A mature member of the staff acts as Head of each boys' camp, and every bungalow has a staff man in charge who lives with the boys.

Junior Camp

Recognizing the need for a different plan in the life of younger boys from that best suited to older ones a separate camp is main-

"Camp is the place where friendships are formed, ideals are generated, character values determined and decisions made which vitally effect life."—H. W. Gibson, Formerly President Camp Directors' Association.

tained for boys nine to fourteen years of age. The camp life is similar to that of the older boys with longer hours of sleep, shorter trips and other modifications to meet the special needs of Juniors.

Middler Camp

The Middler Camp is the largest of the three camps. It meets the needs of boys from thirteen to sixteen years of age.

Senior Camp

The seniors are mature boys from fifteen to nineteen years of age. Their life is more strenuous than that of the other campers and they are allowed to take longer, faster and more difficult trips.

Guest Camp

Parents, guests of the camp, and members of the staff whose wives are at O-wa-kon-ze, are accommodated at the guest camp on the east end of the large island.

Guides' Camp

Separate quarters are maintained for guides, cooks and the camp caretaker.

The Camp Life

On arrival at camp the boys are assigned to a camp home in one of the cabins. The assignments are made with considerable care. If changes are desirable they are made later.

As soon as the trunks have been moved to the cabins, and the boys having donned their camp clothes have had their city clothes carefully labeled and put away on clothes hangers in the camp storeroom provided for this purpose, the regular life of the camp begins.

A general assembly is held at once, a talk is given on safety, introductions are made, the few simple camp rules emphasized. During the first few days through a well planned system of instruction, lectures and demonstrations, the boys are taught the best methods of camping. Difficult and thorough tests in swimming and paddling must be satisfactorily passed before the boys are allowed to go in a canoe without a staffman.

When these tests are finished short trial trips are taken. "Sections" are then formed. A section is a party of twelve containing two to four staffmen and is the O-wa-kon-ze camping trip unit. In forming these sections due consideration is given to the age, strength

"Health is the best formula for happiness."
—Dr. Herman N. Bundeson.

Our Program is Varied, Healthy, Happy

and camping ability of the boys and their preference for companions and leaders.

The trips taken last from a day to a month and are varied in length, speed and difficulty to meet the needs of each group of boys. The trips are so arranged that at intervals the entire camp is together for two or three days. These are big days at O-wa-kon-ze. There are thrilling tales of adventure, of fish and big game. There is a busy time in the photographic studio. There are band and orchestra concerts, vaudeville and motion picture shows, regattas, swimming meets and athletic sports.

The boys' program alternates between the fascinating trip life of adventure and exploration and the highly developed life at the permanent camp where sports, music, shows, photography, musketry, tutoring, camp craft, nature study, first aid, Red Cross life saving courses, building projects and regular coaching courses are major activities.

Activities at the Permanent Camp

Swimming

Much is made of this sport which is very carefully planned and supervised. As an extra precaution the "Buddy System" is used during the swimming periods. There are two swimming periods each day. If a boy seems to be getting too much swimming his periods are limited. Instruction is given in all strokes and the boys are encouraged in every way to improve.

The Red Cross Life Saving Course is given each year by a Red Cross Life Saving Examiner and the official Red Cross Life Saving Emblems awarded to the boys who pass the tests.

Frequent swimming meets are held. There is an enclosed pool, two diving towers and three springboards. There is a sand beach near the camp and another is being built right in the center of the camp. During the swimming periods the boys are given canoes to play with, to upset and right in the water so that they will become thoroughly accustomed to them, and in case of possible accident will not lose their heads. The water toboggan slide is a continual source of exciting good times.

Aviators

Other Aquatic Sports

Frequent regattas are held. Events include rowing races, single, double and "mojo" canoe races, tail end races, gunwale races, tilting, etc. The older boys are taught to manage a sailboat. Instruction and practice is given in the four-oared racing shell. Aquaplaning and water baseball are popular sports.

Athletic and Gymnasium Sports

Teams are organized, coaching given and schedules run in various athletic games. We play basketball, baseball, volley ball, playground ball, soccer, handball, tennis, quoits, paddle tennis, etc.

"Life in the open, good leadership and a spirit of comaraderie, tend to awaken new interests in the child, to discover and overcome weaknesses of character and to encourage latent talents."—Editorial Cosmopolitan Magazine.

Boys Are Trained in the Arts of Self Defense

Expert instruction is given in musketry, and rifle practice is carried on under careful supervision.

Instruction is also given in the use of the tramplin table, in tumbling, tight rope walking and other gymnastic stunts.

The attempt is made to find and teach each boy something in the athletic line in which he can distinguish himself, and to teach him to excel in and enjoy some forms of sport which he will continue for health and pleasure in after years. Special stress is put on sports which the boys have been unable to enjoy during the school year.

Boxing and Wrestling

A knowledge of the arts of self-defense is an important part of a boy's education. As most boys have no opportunity for instruction in these sports considerable attention is given them at O-wa-kon-ze. Boxing and wrestling are taught all campers.

At the close of camp, tournaments are held and prizes given in various sports.

Music

Considerable attention is given to music in the camp, both vocal and instrumental. Instruction is given on all instruments. Boys should bring their instruments with them. The camp owns two pianos, an organ and all the larger instruments necessary to a band. There is a camp orchestra. When talent is plentiful a band is organized. Camp singing is conducted at meals, at evening camp-fires and on special occasions and is very popular. The music adds much to the pleasure of the camp.

Photography

The photographic studio is provided with up-to-date apparatus. There is room and equipment for sixteen boys to work at a time. The boys are taught how to take, develop, print and enlarge pictures. Chemicals for developing and printing are furnished free. An expert in this line of work is in charge of the studio.

Entertainments

Entertainments planned and participated in by boys and staff are given every time the entire camp is together. Each cabin or trip section is usually held responsible for one act of the show. This gives the boys a chance to appear before an audience, brings out hidden talent and develops ingenuity.

In the Junior Camp entertainments around the camp fire are planned for almost every night when there is no special activity planned for all the camps. For the most part these are planned and conducted entirely by the boys and consist of debates, story

Boxing is Stressed

telling contests, riddle contests, contests in magic, in short sketches, rope tying contests and other contests between cabins. All cabins are entered, all boys take part. They do surprisingly well. They show a great deal of resourcefulness and ingenuity and develop a confidence and an assurance in speaking or performing before an audience that is quite unusual.

Library

The camp library contains several hundred volumes of fine books for boys.

"The summer camp is an institution bridging the gap between the school years for the education of mind and body in the outdoors."—Dr. Herbert Trant, Johns Hopkins Medical School.

This space unintentionally left blank

Happy Days
at
O-wa-kon-ze

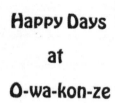

Many Varsity Players Have Been Developed Here

Off for a Trip

Hitting the Water at End of 120-foot Toboggan Slide

Happy Boys at O-wa-kon-ze

Two Good Tennis Courts

Fish and Game Abound

Our Natatorium

Crew Practice

Ready for the Canoe Tests

Where
Health and
Joy Abound

Water Sports are Popular

Equipped for Everything Boys Like to Do

Boys Are Taught to Sail

Campers Live in Comfortable Cabins

Expert Coaching in All Sports

Camp Duties

The boys are required to keep their quarters neat and clean. A rigid inspection is made each morning. The boys take turns at waiting on their own table, are placed on various committees having responsibility for the conduct of the affairs of the camp, and are occasionally assigned to other jobs which present themselves. Camp improvements are being made continually and afford a wide range of experience in the use of tools, construction of frame and log buildings, piers, concrete mixing, repairs of canoes, boats and engines, installation and repair of electrical supplies and plumbing, and ingenious methods of handling heavy logs, boats, machinery, etc. In these activities the boys are encouraged to take part. They are usually very much interested and the training and experience is valuable.

Tutoring

Tutoring is given in preparatory school subjects and in music. The charge is $3.00 per hour for school subjects, $2.00 per half hour lesson in music.

Fish and Big Game Abound

Casting

The art of casting is taught at the camp. The camp has a set of the regular tournament casting rings and some fine tournament casting outfits that all boys are privileged to use. The regulation casting plugs without hooks are used. To avoid the possibility of stepping on hooks no casting with hooks is allowed from the camp property. The casting pool is directly in front of the administration buildings. This has proved to be a fascinating sport. Tournaments are held and a golf game played over the five ring course.

An O-wa-kon-ze Bear

Fishing and Hunting

Baril Lake is the natural home of lake trout, whitefish, pickerel and great northern pike. Whitefish can be caught only with a net. The others are easily taken with hook and line at all times. Baril Lake was stocked with wall-eyed pike in 1928 and with speckled trout in 1929. Nearby lakes and streams will be stocked with other game fish as fast as fry can be obtained.

Fine bass fishing is found on the trips but we have found none close to camp. Bass and rainbow trout have been planted in Mille Lacs but this is a large lake and we have not yet found where they are. Great northern pike are found in all lakes and run to forty-five pounds in weight.

Ontario fishing licenses cost $5.50. These can be purchased at the camp. The fishing is remarkably fine and all boys want licenses. There is an extra charge of $5.00 in the Quetico.

Hunting is confined to the camera as all game is out of season until September 1st. The boys are not allowed to have firearms in their possession. Game, however, is seen continually. Moose and deer are plentiful. Beaver, muskrat, mink and fisher are quite common. Foxes, wolves and bear are seen frequently. The woods teem with partridge and rabbits. Many kinds of ducks and other wild fowl are seen. There are no poisonous snakes.

"The summer camp deserves a prominent place in education because of the large contribution it is making toward the development of stalwart, upright and loyal citizens."—Dr. Geo. L. Meylan, Columbia University.

The Club House

Game Building

Rainy Days

Attired in camp clothes and accustomed to outdoor life we pay little attention to the light drizzles which keep us indoors in the city. Camp activities go on as usual. For the occasional really bad day there are many things to keep the boys occupied and happy. The bungalows are comfortable and roomy. The big clubhouse is a pleasant place to be. It contains a huge fireplace around which the campers love to gather and is an ideal place for entertainments. Chess, checkers, pingpong and many other games are popular. The large new game building is also attractively furnished for all kinds of indoor games. A shelter has been built at the rifle range so that this activity can be carried on in inclement weather. This is a good time for music, photography, letter writing and reading. An entertainment or lecture is usually planned for the evening.

Sundays

Sunday at camp is a day of rest and quiet recreation. A song service is held in the morning.

Letters Home

Boys are required to write to their parents once a week. When on trips a letter must be written just before departure and another upon return to camp.

Commissariat

Many think this is the place where the most important camp activities occur. This department is in charge of an expert cook and his assistants. An abundance of good, wholesome, well cooked food is supplied. Fresh milk, fresh meat and fresh vegetables are staple articles of diet. Good railroad service, refrigerator cars and a well filled icehouse make this possible. The menu is worked out by an expert dietitian.

Banquet

The camp banquet is held on the last night in camp. It is served in regular banquet style. The dining-hall is beautifully decorated with pine boughs and ferns. The women guests of the camp act as waitresses. There is music by the camp orchestra. Appropriate speeches and awards are made.

The Best of Food

"The education that is real is the education that means our being of finer temper, more adaptable, more flexible."—James Ramsay McDonald.

Trips

Good fishing is found throughout the district. Big game is seen not occasionally, but continually, on the trips. Four moose and a bear may be seen in the picture on the left.

Plenty of Thrills on the Trips

Juniors Visiting an Indian Camp

LEFT—Wet Feet, but Colds are Unknown

"Our national health is our greatest asset."—Theodore Roosevelt.

Awards

The attractive camp athletic emblem is awarded to boys who make the camp teams. The O-wa-kon-ze medal is given for the best work in photography, marksmanship, swimming, canoeing, tennis, boxing, wrestling, handball and quoits. Fine silver cups are awarded to the Junior, Middler and Senior who are considered to be the best campers. The boys, themselves, determine the winner by a separate vote on each one of the following qualifications:

Camp spirit, loyalty, determination, honesty and fairness, clean speech and good manners, willingness and helpfulness, unselfishness and generosity, courage and self-reliance, common sense, responsibility, self-control, ambition, initiative, industriousness, perseverance, punctuality, life, energy, vigor, alertness, good fellowship and good nature, fair play and good sportsmanship.

The CANOE TRIPS and REAL CAMPING throughout this IDEAL CAMPING COUNTRY are the most outstanding features at O-wa-kon-ze. They at once distinguish this camp from the many so-called "camps" located on crowded lakes in summer resort districts. O-wa-kon-ze campers are completely away from the disadvantages of city and society life. They get REAL CAMPING EXPERIENCE. The district through which the trips go is rugged and wild, untouched by civilization. Much of it is unexplored. There are thousands of beautiful lakes and streams. Hundreds are not shown on any map. The life makes a great appeal to the desire to explore, the desire for adventure inherent in every boy.

The canoes used on the trips are all seventeen and eighteen foot "guide models," the safest and best model for cruising. The boys travel, usually, three in a canoe. The guide's canoe leads. One of the staff is always in the rear canoe. The canoes are kept fairly close together. The guides are naturally cautious. They pick the channels, select the camping sites, skirt the shores to keep out of high winds and assume a large share of the responsibility for the safety and success of the trips.

The boy learns from the guides and experienced campers how to meet the conditions of primitive life and to make himself and others comfortable under those conditions. In a short time he picks up from them the camping "kinks" which most sportsmen have acquired only after years of hardship and many disastrous and unpleasant experiences. These camping adventures are what the boy most enjoys and are the things he will love to talk about years after his O-wa-kon-ze experience is only a memory.

At O-wa-kon-ze the trips are a regular part of the camp life. No extra charge is made for them except when the trip entails extra and unusual expense, such as railroad fare, express of canoes, etc., as happens occasionally when part of a trip is made on the train. This expense is prorated among the boys. These items, however, are insignificant.

The Trip Life Appeals to All Boys

"I have found that the impressions which a man receives by the brookside, or in the forest, make him a better man and a better citizen; nearness to nature has an elevating influence on heart and character." — Grover Cleveland.

Safety

"SAFETY FIRST" is the watchword of the camp. The first camp lecture is on safety. All camp activities are carefully supervised to insure safety. Members of the staff are expert swimmers. They are experienced campers and are alert to avert danger. The trips are conducted by competent staffmen and experienced guides. Boys are not allowed to overdo. First aid kits are a part of the trip outfit.

The Red Cross Life Saving course, the First Aid course, the "Buddy" and O. D. systems, the careful supervision of a large and competent staff (always on the job, there being no outside attractions in this uninhabited region to divide their attention) all make for the safety of the camp.

One of the older staffmen acts each day as officer of the day. No one is allowed to use a boat or leave camp without his permission. A record is kept of all boys who leave camp. This record contains the boy's name, his companions' names, the number of the canoe or boat, where he is going and when he will return. On their return the boys are required to report back to the O. D.

Medical Supervision

In case of accident or illness professional care is always at hand. The camp sanitation is in charge of the camp physician who supervises all matters pertaining to the health of the boys and gives lectures on hygiene and first aid. Each boy is given a thorough medical examination on arrival at camp, at the middle and at the end of the season. A record is kept of the conditions observed. Modifications of exercise, bathing, rest and diet are made when deemed desirable to secure the best results in health and normal development.

Nutrition is carefully watched. Boys who are under weight are given milk between meals and may have their activities restricted. Special attention is given the care of the teeth. We invite the co-operation of the family physician. Any particular care which the boy needs should be reported.

Rest Hour

The camp has a rest hour immediately after the noon meal.

Hospital

A hospital cabin is always ready should an emergency arise. Should it be necessary a boy can be transported to a first class hospital at Port Arthur or International Falls. All trains are stopped for us in cases of emergency. These are valuable safeguards. There has never been a serious accident, and illness is practically unknown at the camp. Every precaution is taken, however, and we try to foresee and provide for any emergencies which may arise.

Laundry

The camp laundry supplies weekly laundry service which the boys are required to take advantage of. A charge of $10.00 will be made all boys for this service.

Mail, Telegraph, Express

Mail, express and telegrams should be addressed to Owakonze Camps, Ltd., Owakonze, Ontario.

Parents and friends are not encouraged to send packages to camp as they are held for duty at the border, necessitating considerable delay and inconvenience. The duty is usually quite heavy. Candy and cake must not be sent or brought to the boys. This has probably caused more sickness in camps than all other causes combined. Customs officials will be asked to return all such packages to sender.

Special Parties

The camp arranges outings and trips for families or groups of men who wish to spend all or part of their vacation in this district. Guides are furnished all groups which go out from camp on long trips. Guides for these parties can usually be obtained only upon long notice. For their services guests will be asked to pay a wage of $6.00 a day, their expenses to and from camp and their board at the rate of $10.00 a week. The camp fee for guests is $12.00 per week. All supplies are furnished by the camp. Arrangements must be made well in advance.

"It is during the growing years, while both mind and body are plastic that children learn how best to occupy their leisure time, so as [...] the neglect of exercise and recreation."—Dr. R. Tait McKenzie, Univ. of Pennsylvania.

W. L. Childs

THE director and his wife are at the camp throughout the season.

Mr. W. L. Childs, Director of the camp, has had over twenty years of experience in training boys as a director of physical education, athletic coach and as camp director. In 1907 he was director of a Y. M. C. A. camp of 100 boys and has been connected for twenty years with various boys' camps.

He is a member of the Camp Directors' Association of America and was one of the founders of the Mid West Camp Directors' Association.

He studied at the University of Chicago, at Yale and at Harvard, and received his technical training at the Chicago Association College.

Mr. Childs has had marked success as an athletic coach. He coached the basket ball and gymnastic teams at the University of Chicago for three years, giving his alma mater her first conference basket ball championship.

For the past twenty-one years he has been Head of the Department of Physical Education at New Trier High School, Winnetka, Ill., where he holds the confidence of the community from which most of the campers of the O-wa-kon-ze Camps are drawn.

Staff

The staff includes men of mature age, teachers and athletic coaches, experienced campers and experienced in dealing with boys, and younger men, selected for their personality, their ideals, their skill in athletics and experience in camping. They are the type of man to inspire in boys hero worship and high ideals.

Men in charge of the various activities are experts in their line. Changes in the personnel of the staff make it impossible to give a correct list of the staff at the time camp booklets must go to press. Most camps print the staff of the previous season. We prefer to issue a separate bulletin at a later date giving the correct information.

There will be at least one man to every five boys. As far as possible we retain on the staff the experienced men who have had an important part in making the O-wa-kon-ze Camps a really worthwhile chapter in the lives of boys. The utmost care is used in the selection of the staff, and we are constantly awake to every opportunity to raise the standard of the camp staff.

The Cabin Heads are men who understand boys and are sympathetic and friendly. The heads of the three camps are school men who have had many years of successful experience in teaching and training boys.

A Personnel Director in co-operation with the Program Directors works through the Camp Heads and Cabin Heads in making a study of each boy, in helping the boy to solve his problems and in adjusting contacts and program to best meet each boy's needs.

The Trip to Camp

The trip to camp and return is made in the camp's special train via the Chicago and Northwestern Railway from Chicago to Duluth, and the Canadian National Railway from Duluth to Owakonze. The best of service and every courtesy is extended to our campers by these transportation companies. The trip takes about twenty-two hours each way. The group from St. Paul and Minneapolis joins the main party at Duluth. Full instructions regarding tickets, baggage, etc., will be sent to parents about June 1st.

Parents and Guests

Parents and guests are always welcome but must make reservations well in advance. The guest fee is $6.00 per day. Guests live in cabins and in comfortable house tents at a separate camp but have their meals in the large main dining room.

Many guests come by rail through Fort Frances, but most of them prefer to take the Northern Navigation boat or the bus from Duluth to Port Arthur or motor to Port Arthur and take the Canadian National train from there to Owakonze. The boat trip is a delightful one and the Scott Highway from Duluth to Port Arthur through the Superior National Forest is a beautiful drive. The trip from Port Arthur to camp must be made by train as there are no auto roads through our camping country.

Guests going all the way by train should take advantage of the thirty day summer tourist fare. Full details regarding the trip may be obtained from Mr. Noble M. Kean of the Northwestern City Ticket Office, Chicago.

"My idea of a University is Mark Hopkins on one end of a log and a student on the other."—James A. Garfield.

Invest for Your Boy—Don't Let Him Waste the Summer

Such a camp experience should be considered not merely as a happy outing but as the finest possible investment for the boy; an investment in growth, health, vitality, education, in ability to make friends and the development of qualities, ideals, right habits of living and joyful ways of employing leisure time which will net the boy large returns in success and happiness all his life long. No similar period in his school year approaches the value of this camp experience to the boy. Don't let the boy waste the summer. It should be to him the most valuable period of the whole year. And don't wait until he is too old. The best results are obtained with boys under 16 and the 9th year is a good year to start.

The Camp Season

Eight weeks beginning the first week in July.

Terms

The fee is $325.00 for the full term of eight weeks. The camp fee for guests is $42.00 per week.

Camp fees must be paid in advance. An enrollment fee of $50.00 must accompany the application. The remaining $275.00 is due June first and must be paid before the camp season opens.

After an application has been accepted there can be no abatement of charges allowed for cancellation, late arrival, withdrawal or dismissal.

Besides the cost of the trip to camp, the camp fee and an inexpensive personal outfit, the only additional expenses should be duffle bag, tump line and paddle, $12.00; Ontario fishing license, $5.50; Quetico fishing license, $5.00; laundry, $10.00, and expense of stamps, stationery, fishing tackle, photography, tutoring and sometimes a small charge for transportation as when part of a trip is made by railroad. Entire cost of summer need not be over $425.00.

What to Take to Camp

Old but serviceable clothing, stout shoes (12-inch moccasin boots recommended), 3 pairs long khaki trousers, a dark colored sweater, tennis shoes, sox, flannel shirts (lumber jack shirts popular), white cotton track shirts and shorts for underwear, pajamas (preferably flannel), white handkerchiefs, bandana handkerchief, towels, ivory soap, comb, toothbrush, toothpaste, two small laundry bags, bathing suit, bath robe, basket ball suit, raincoat, writing material (no U. S. postage), two good books for camp library, needles and thread, two pillow cases, one small pillow (may be rented at camp $1.00), three pairs of heavy wool blankets or one pair of light blankets and one pair of four point Hudson's Bay blankets or instead of blankets one Owakonze sleeping bag to be purchased from the Mohican Spinning Co., Peru, Indiana at $16.50. These bags should be ordered by the middle of June. They are quite satisfactory.

Two small bags for toilet articles, etc., paddle, tump line, duffle bag, lumbermen's heavy wool sox, and blanket pins are necessary articles and should be purchased at the camp. Hudson's Bay blankets may be purchased from the camp at Canadian rates. Order well in advance.

A camera, fishing tackle (short rod, reel, line, hooks, bass and musky spoons size 4 to 9), books, games, writing material, musical instruments, compass, Boy Scout knife, flashlight, tennis racquet and baseball glove are desirable but not essential articles.

The above list is quite complete.

On their first trip boys usually bring a lot of expensive and useless equipment. The camp store carries a full line of carefully selected camp and photographic supplies. Purchasing at the camp will insure getting the right thing at a reasonable price and will avoid difficulties of purchase, transportation and duty.

All articles of clothing should be plainly marked with woven name tapes. Blank for ordering will be sent to parents.

Only small steamer trunks should be taken. To insure their being put on the camp train trunks should be sent to Chicago a day ahead. As trunk keys are often lost a duplicate key should be deposited with Mr. Childs. Baggage is inspected by Customs Officials at the border. Patrons of the camp receive every courtesy.

The Summer Camp by Walter Camp

"These camps create a love and appreciation of the out-of-doors. They open a new vista to the city boy and instill in him the lure of the open trail. They develop the 'molly coddle' into a boy who can face wind and weather and hardship without a whimper. They produce initiative by teaching a boy to do things for himself. They develop resourcefulness by bringing the boy back more nearly to primitive conditions. They inculcate co-operation and sportsmanship and teach the boy to think unselfishly, to render all the help he can, and to advance not himself but his community."—Cosmopolitan.

Letters of Appreciation from Patrons of the Camp

(The following quotations are unsolicited recommendations. Names and addresses furnished on request.)

"Sending Bob to O-WA-KON-ZE was the best investment I ever made."

"James got more out of his summer at O-WA-KON-ZE than he ever received from an entire year at school."

"My son, after spending two seasons with you, says 'I would rather spend my vacations at Camp O-WA-KON-ZE than any other place. The camp spirit is fine, plenty of good wholesome food, varied sports and every boy has the time of his life. Yes, we come home as hard as knots'."

"Franklin had a most wonderful time and came back so greatly benefited and hardened that I cannot help but feel that he has been enabled to stand the strain of intensive school work. He went to O-WA-KON-ZE a tired, nervous boy and came back hard as nails.

"Both Mrs. Bowes and I feel very grateful to you, not only for the wonderful time he had, but for helping to give him a good health foundation."

"The last two seasons have been of great pleasure and profit to my boys and a matter of great satisfaction to their father, and I trust they cannot only get the same experience this summer but give their best for the benefit of the camp in general and the newcomers in particular."

"Our boy came home from camp in fine condition and fifteen pounds heavier in weight than at the beginning of vacation. We very much appreciate the benefits he received from his summer in the wilds."

"Davidson returned safe and sound and looking exceedingly well."

"Mrs. Sommers and I look back with a great deal of pleasure to the week that we spent with you and hope at some time to have a chance to live it over again."

"Both Mrs. ———— and myself are greatly pleased at the results of our boy's summer at O-WA-KON-ZE. It did a great deal for him in many ways and we greatly appreciate your work and interest in the young man, which effected a really remarkable change in his attitude on many subjects. I hope some day our younger boy may have the opportunity of attending O-WA-KON-ZE."

"Frederick had a thoroughly good time and one that we feel was profitable to him. He surely has enjoyed his summer. He wrote his father, 'Talk of your good times, I've got them all beat,' and not a complaint of anything has crept into his letters."

"We want you to know that we approve of the methods of conducting the camp."

"I can't help but mention the fact that your staff of men in charge could not be improved, each man fitted for his particular duties. You also have a fine group of boys, every one a gentleman, we enjoyed them all."

"I have never seen a place where the conditions were so ideal for the development of manly qualities in boys."

"We feel sure Frank will be as happy at O-WA-KON-ZE as our other boys have been, and hope he will blossom out there as much as Charles did. Charles always loved the camp and we are glad he is to be there again."

"We are receiving wonderful letters from both boys. They are surely having the time of their lives."

What the Campers Say About Owakonze

"If I lived a thousand years I couldn't finish telling of the good times I've had."

"If there is a finer camp in the U. S. or Canada, then I am from Missouri and will have to be shown it."

"I think that Owakonze is as good a camp (even better), than there ever was, is or will be. I think any improvement will be impossible."

"If you are going to do anything for the average man you have got to begin before he is a man. The chance of success lies in working with the boy and not with the man."
—Theodore Roosevelt.

Boyhood passes quickly. Soon it will be too late. To be sure of a place in the camp, enrollment should be made very early. Mail application below at once.

Postscript

Our thanks to Allison Ickes Dalton who was very kind to let us publish Don's "Reminiscences of Owakonze" on the occasion of the 2016 Owakonze Reunion.

As the erstwhile publisher of this volume I am taking the liberty of adding a Don Ickes story of my own. I worked for Don for three summers on the work crew and learned so much from him. He mentored me on no end of interesting tasks; from building the A Frame, to cleaning out the massive lint trap under the laundry, to blowing up rocks on the portage road with dynamite. Don was almost always patient with the raucous, smart mouthed, testosterone brimming young men who comprised the work crew. (and when he blew up we had earned it!)

While there are hundreds of stories of how Don ingeniously solved problems I will share just one that sums it up.

At the opening of a camp season I appeared from the Portage with a large wooden trunk marked, "Postmaster". "Aha," Don exclaimed, "It's the Postmaster supply trunk!" The trunk was locked and Don's standard Postal key would not open it. We slit open the letter attached to the trunk and learned, "The trunk keys have been changed. The key to the trunk is in the mailbag that arrived with the trunk." Unfortunately the key to unlock the mailbag was in the locked trunk!

Don said, "Well Terry, you will just have to cut open the mailbag." I protested that I could not as he had previously instructed me that damaging a malibag was a federal offense. "No," he said, "it would be an even greater offense for the Postmaster to do it. but we can leave no evidence of YOUR crime." So I was given my instructions. "Slit open the mailbag and remove the key. Then take the mailbag down near the powerhouse, soak it in gasoline and then burn it. Take the lock and chain out into the middle of the lake and sink them."

I followed his instructions and it has remained an unsolved crime till this day.

Terry Jones 59-70

Donald Wilmarth Ickes
September 23, 1924-January 16, 1995

Published by Satisfaction Works Ltd. Press 2016
This original work has been revised and
extended with additional photographs
and the 1930 Owakonze brochure

A REAL CAMP FOR BOYS AND MEN

CAMP
O·WA·KON·ZE

BARIL LAKE
ONTARIO, CANADA

Made in United States
North Haven, CT
26 August 2022

23290681R00076